GW01315942

The Layman's Guide to the New Age

THE
LAYMAN'S
GUIDE
to the
NEW AGE

SCRIBED BY
PETER
RHODES-DIMMER

ILLUSTRATED
BY
NICHOLAS SMITH

CADUCEUS

© PETER RHODES-DIMMER
Velma Boathouse
Broom Close
Teddington
Middlesex
TW11 9RL
UK

Published by CADUCEUS PUBLISHING,1992

ISBN 1 897637 00 4

All rights reserved. No part of this publication may be reproduced, stored in a retrieval system, or transmitted in any form by any means, electronic, mechanical, phoyocopying, recording or otherwise, without the prior permission of Peter Rhodes-Dimmer.

Designed and illustrated by
Nicholas Smith
Text output by Angel Graphics
Produced by Mandarin Offset
Printed in Hong Kong

This book is dedicated to the ending of World Hunger and the restoration and recovery of our environment.

ACKNOWLEDGEMENTS

The following people have helped me greatly with preparing 'The Layman's Guide to the New Age' and I would therefore like to acknowledge :-

HILARY NEWMAN for her part in the original inspiration,

JILL SINGER for being a fearless and able editor, and in helping to consolidate many passages of the book in the early stages,

GILL BRIGHTEN for many hours of support,

MOIRA for her dramatic channelling, which was the basis for a whole section,

DAVID HADDA for his excellent advice (not always taken) on good use of English,

CHRISSY MERTON for her meticulous proof reading,

OONAH HARPUR for checking and debating several sections with love and integrity.

My thanks to you all.

Peter Rhodes-Dimmer

CONTENTS

INTRODUCTION

Many ancient writings including the Bible, the Koran and the commentaries of Nostradamus point to the end of the 20th century as being the culmination of a planetary age and the dawning of a new era.

More recently, the great Albert Einstein, writing in the 1940's, predicted mathematically that the rate of change of human learning was in the process of becoming exponential. He concluded that this would lead our species to change radically and that the change would be of the mind rather than the physical body.

All these predictions are now rapidly drawing together as the New Age - the Age of Aquarius - commences ....

To help you absorb some of the exciting new ideas set out in this book, I recommend an addition to your personal way of thinking. The technique I suggest gives you a powerful new tool for understanding. It is called 'Possibility Consciousness'.

We human beings are taught from an early age to judge every statement that is presented to us - to categorise them in terms of 'yes' or 'no', acceptance or rejection. So many issues of spirituality cannot be proven in scientific terms, and our training leads us to reject them automatically. What option do we have? Totally and publicly embracing the esoteric is likely to leave you with little credibility.

The fact remains that there is so much 'circumstantial' evidence of the paranormal that, if you look at all closely it is difficult to deny that something is happening.

'Possibility Consciousness' allows you to hold together in your mind all the unproven spiritual and supernatural phenomena which you experience, or which interests you, in a way that accepts them as a possibility. Treat it as a separate storage area in the mind. In this area of your consciousness you can build up material you wish to work with, while not having to judge it. You simply hold it as being possible.

You will then find that a surprising number of spiritual and paranormal issues begin to link together to form strong patterns and synergies in your mind. You will also start to remember....

The text you are about to read has serious work to do in helping to bring about the things that are predicted for that New Age. This book has the specific purpose of achieving wide circulation and stirring the interest of people who may otherwise be unaware of the era of dramatic change that humanity is entering.

A small percentage of the world population are well aware of what is going on, and for them this material will serve to confirm - or to integrate - what they already know.

This book is not primarily for them, but for the vast majority of people whose consciousness is only just awakening, or is now ready for progress.

These messages give cause for great optimism, and I hope that you will find they excite you. If you believe the content deserves attention, be a catalyst for change and draw other peoples' attention to it. Do some networking among your friends and acquaintances. Leave it on your coffee table, start discussions about it, give it as a present and encourage others to read it.

I predict that interesting things will happen to you as you introduce people to the book, for its purpose is to stimulate change and encourage personal growth. If you wish to write and share your experiences with me, I shall be delighted to hear about them!

Peter Rhodes-Dimmer
London, 1992.

A BRIEF ACCOUNT OF HOW THIS BOOK HAPPENED

Although I was the 'scribe' for this document, and have done a great deal of work to make it cohesive, most of the material was not generated by me: it was channelled from elsewhere. For those readers who do not know about channelling, it is a little like the act of being a medium, but without the crystal ball and mystical environment, and, at least for me, not in the form of a consultation with another human being.

Some well known people with the ability to channel claim to have a close relationship and communication with one or more advanced spiritual beings, who they know by name. There are others who say that the phenomena result from contacting the 'higher self', and that a sort of deep wisdom from within is being revealed in the process.

I have read of those who have great control over their channelling, but on several of the occasions when it has happened to me it has been insistent to the point of embarrassment. My control of the situation has been zero! Indeed, one of the side effects of the act of channelling is that it makes me very weepy, doing little for my self image as a reasonably macho man!

While the book was being compiled this phenomenon occurred to me on many occasions. One day it happened in a very public situation in a new restaurant, after I had ignored the first signs of another 'delivery' of channelled material . After sitting and weeping in such a public place for some minutes I decided that I was going to have to take more notice, if only to defend my reputation for a reasonable degree of emotional security!

When channelled information comes through I have to transcribe a series of thoughts that appear to be given to me, and which completely dominate my mind until they are on paper. Now, I have learned to get on with it as soon as possible.

Personally, I do not consider myself accomplished as a writer, and neither have I ever thought of myself as particularly spiritual, so the whole process has been a great surprise. Yet since I first became aware of the subject, this sometimes rather eccentric script (or so it appeared as I was writing it) has been insisting that it is written and published.

The real authors are somewhere above us in the Cosmos - it was they who decided that I was to be the vehicle for setting this particular text down, and as the channel, I had little say in the matter, once I had agreed to do the job!

Most of the ideas in this work have been expressed before in many New Age writings, but although there are a surprising number of dedicated people developing their spiritual interest around the world, real focus on the subject is still restricted to a very small percentage of the total population. The fact is that, as the channel for this work, I was completely unaware of most of what is available in print at the time that this work was being written.

The difference is that many of the available writings go, in considerable depth, into a single aspect of what is going on. This one, however, is designed to give an overview, and show the positive things that are developing.

For despite many negative things happening in the World currently, there are positive events and major changes predicted in the immediate future. It is a prerequisite that humanity should become aware of, focus on and embrace concepts of the new age. This new understanding will undoubtably be achieved through many different routes. This work is but one of a large number.

As you become involved with the subject you will be constantly surprised by the high percentage of people around you who are individually optimistic for change in the future. Many of them will already have drawn, and will express, similar conclusions to you about what is developing for humanity. When you talk about what you are discovering, you will find that others are clearly relieved to find they are not alone in what they are beginning to believe.

The text came in four main parts which were later broken into shorter and clearer sections, and their first running orders changed somewhat, during editing. The first elements to arrive consisted of 'The Invitation', 'Fear and Ego' and 'Visitors', and was delivered during a state of heightened awareness resulting from an hour of controlled breathing exercises - incidentally, a wonderful 'high' without any stimulants! Afterwards, I sat at my word processor, typing away without really knowing what was being created.

On first reading the initial three pages of draft I literally exclaimed "Oh my God, what have I written.....?" I did not recognise one word of what had been printed!

The second section resulted from witnessing an extraordinary incident during a weekend workshop on healing. Our woman leader had well established powers as a channel, and towards the end of the day her spirit guide spoke very forcefully through her to the assembled group. Despite her many similar experiences she was visibly shaken by the weight of the message and she remained so for several days. This section, called 'The Earth Warnings', is an accurate condensing of the message her guide sent on that memorable Sunday. It is the only section to have been delivered by a 'third party'.

Some days later, while I was in the shower, the phrase 'Communication is the Key' started to ring insistently in my head, not to be shaken away. Hurrying to the word processor, the paragraphs of 'Communication and Future' and the sections that follow it started to pour onto the page.

The next sections to be delivered were 'Love', 'Intimate Relationships' and 'Parting'. Small phrases buzzed around in my head for many days, and eventually the word 'Paradigm' was the trigger that set off a cohesive first draft. Three pages emerged without any planning or even reading until it was complete.

The final major section caused several sleepless nights, and eventually at 4.40 one morning I gave in, sat up and wrote several pages of scribbled notes. 'Intuition and Creativity', 'Abundance and Wealth', 'Government Aid', and 'World Finance' had been delivered!

With all this verbiage coming together, an experienced Editor was needed. Shortly after making this decision (but having no idea how to proceed), the solution came at a rather pretentious dinner party. When I sat next to a woman who was clearly feeling very bored, she immediately told me "I really don't know what I'm doing here". We talked, and by a marvellous coincidence here was my principal editor, who, with all the right credentials, has since given large amounts of both supportive and objective advice in putting the material into a readable form.

Considerable time has thus been spent editing the work into a cohesive document, and verifying many passages.

The running order has been changed from the sequence in which the passages were originally delivered, and this has added to clarity and impact. Many small sections - sometimes just one paragraph - have been delivered, and integrated into the whole.

Valuable guidance has been given by several people who know the subject matter well, and who have kindly spent time to offer a critique and make helpful comments. However, the writing remains true to the original channelled words, with a small amount added in an effort to give continuity, and, where necessary, a degree of explanation.

As many readers will be new to the whole subject of 'New Age' beliefs, it should be made clear that the total story is much greater than is recorded here. There are many New Age topics, approaches and interpretations, coming from a wide variety of sources, but all pointing in the same direction. This book is specifically intended to focus your interest and suggest ways you may wish to go forward. Once you are started, I believe you will make many exciting new discoveries.

THE POWERS OF THE UNIVERSE

ARE POISED TO TAKE YOU

AND HUMANITY

ON A GREAT ADVENTURE :

IT WILL CHANGE THE WORLD

AND ALL AROUND YOU

YOUR HELP IS NEEDED

BUT FIRST

YOU MUST FIND YOURSELF.

THE
INVITATION

YOU ARE INVITED on a journey : to join many of your fellow human beings who are embarking on an adventure of self-discovery.

A NEW WORLD renaissance is gaining momentum : you are to be a part of it.

THIS NEW AGE is a time of expanding consciousness and spiritual freedom : we are discovering the true purpose of our being here.

EXCITEMENT and fulfilment will come into your life when you explore these new life possibilities.

BY ACCEPTING the invitation you will enhance personal growth and :

ACHIEVE peace with yourself in all things, yet be more effective in the conduct of your life -

DISCOVER ways to eliminate your fears and insecurities -

GROW in spiritual stature without needing organised religion -

DEVELOP your creative skills to increase wealth and happiness -

ESTABLISH your real purpose in being here -

CEASE struggling with your progress in life.

NEW CONSCIOUSNESS will show you a greater potential for humanity than you ever imagined.

BY sharing your experiences with others you will help invoke global change : a great leap forward in mind, spirit and understanding.

THE RESULTS will be dramatic:

FOR WHEN this new perspective becomes widely acknowledged, the world will achieve permanent metamorphosis.

NOT ONLY will every human being be fed, clothed and securely housed : no-one will starve or go hungry.

BUT THERE will be wealth enough to achieve a standard of living for all, at a level that few have yet attained.

PEOPLE will be valued for their differences, and their cultural richness : not for their conformity.

GOVERNMENT will steadily devolve upwards so that global issues are handled globally : war will become a thing of the past.

BUT HUMANITY'S desire to embrace new possibilities must first reach a critical mass.

ENOUGH OF HUMANITY

MUST BELIEVE.

YOU ARE INVITED to explore what is happening, test for yourself what is possible for you, and take action.

COMMIT TO ENTHUS-ING your family, friends, community and all that are around you : they are all needed to help invoke this vital change.

BECOME first and foremost a citizen of the world : take action for its progress.

A PAINFUL PROGRESSION

WE SPEND our lives chasing a false vision of progress : we seek material wealth without seeing the need for spiritual growth.

STRUGGLING at great personal cost, we move slowly and painfully forward, often in the wrong direction.

WE ISOLATE OURSELVES from the lessons of life by putting up barriers : insularity, over-commitment to business or a frantic social life.

IN SO DOING we create a block-age to our perceptions.

THE degree to which we avoid what is going on around us is the degree to which we avoid learning and push away progress in life itself.

BY FAILING to learn vital lessons, pain becomes inevit-able. Each lesson is repeated many times, each more forceful than the last: eventually we get the point, graduate from class, and move on.

LIFE can become so painful for some that they cannot wait to leave : but avoidance of our lessons is not why we came, the extreme of sui-cide not a valid exit route.

IF WE AVOID the issues we were sent here to learn, we will simply come back to start all over again.

*E*VERY experience we have in life reflects the state of our consciousness : we draw situations to us in order to learn and make progress.

*T*HE CRISES, problems and extremes of behaviour we experience are always purposeful : those things we cannot love and accept about ourselves are merely being reflected back to us.

*S*TANDING in judgement and allocating blame for the situations we encounter causes us to learn nothing : therefore, in every difficulty you meet, ask yourself what you are learning.

*T*HE WAY FORWARD is to embrace and deal with your problems as they arise.

*B*Y GREETING every aspect of life with love and acceptance, you disarm each potential problem.

*Y*OU THEN LEARN the lesson quickly and move on, removing pain from the process.

*R*EAL PROGRESS LIES in the growth of spirit and understanding, and for that we must prepare.

S O U L

THERE ARE POWERFUL and intelligent energy beings that span the universe. Their purpose is creation : they are at a far higher level than humanity.

THE SPARK OF LIFE that drives you is that same energy : it is immortal.

YOU ARE NOT MERELY the physical body which you experience now : for we each exist in many dimensions way beyond the physical.

YOUR TRUE IDENTITY is hidden from you by the illusions and demands of life on earth.

THE LIFE ENERGY that is personal to you is called your soul : it is the essence of who you really are.

THE SOUL exists in many states- within a human body; as a spirit being free to explore space and time; and as a part of universal consciousness.

THESE EXISTENCES are all happening in the now : you are connected to all of them.

EACH OF US is here in human form as a volunteer.

WHEN you first came to earth it was seen by the energy beings of the universe as a great privilege to occupy a human body.

YOUR SOUL on earth has since passed through many lives and has great experience : along the way you have made choices and set directions for your growth and progress.

FOR YOU ARE UNIQUE in the universe as a physical creature of absolute choice and great spiritual potential.

*Y*OU ARE HERE to grow and eventually fulfil the true human design : for many, the task of lifetimes is nearing completion.

*B*EFORE YOU CAME to this present life you decided your purpose, your friends : and the lessons that you would learn while you were here.

*O*N ARRIVAL you forgot your plan, as we all do : yet the knowledge is still buried deep in your consciousness, and you can recall it.

23

WE ARE the universe's great experiment to create the perfect marriage between the physical and the spiritual : you chose to come here to be a part of it.

NOTHING about your progress is predestined. Only one being is responsible for your progress : that is you!

THE WORLD is our school for our spiritual progress : you will eventually rise above it to a higher plane. But for now, there are lessons still to be learnt.

YOUR SOUL was given impressive facilities for its time here : your body as its physical environment, your intellect as a powerful capacity to think and rationalise.

YOUR spirituality is provided as a communications link to humanity, to the beings of the universe and thus to higher truth.

THE soul must develop : therefore it creates many learning situations for you along the way.

IT ATTRACTS that which it loves, and also that which it secretly fears : in the former it finds a mirror for itself and the latter is a constant source of learning until fear is eliminated.

TWO OR MORE SOULS may sometimes seek to inhabit the same body, leading to great personal insecurity, extremes of behaviour, and mental illness.

SOME SOULS of thoses who have died and are temporarily free of body are reluctant to move forward in their development : they can sometimes take over another human being, uninvited.

A WEAK SOUL may invite another to share one body by virtue of its specific needs : the physical being is then said to be possessed, and will show signs of split personality.

A STRONG SOUL may capture that of a close friend or relative at their death, and refuse to let them go.

THE RESULT will be rising agitation and aggressiveness of the physical host, perhaps over many years, as the loved one struggles to be set free and move on.

WE ARE CONDITIONED to see these phenomena as mental illness or personality disorders.

YET they can be a pure conflict between souls, and require appropriate resolution : the weak soul must eventually grow, the loved one be freed.

THE HUMAN BEING who is released by being exorcised will change dramatically, free to start developing again without hindrance.

AEONS OF EXISTENCE here on earth have distanced humanity from understanding its true origins, its purpose and its commitments.

NOW, YOUR SOUL will start to gently remind you : you will begin to remember who you really are.

AS YOUR SOUL GROWS, your connections to the world of energy beings will be restored, and you will understand.

PURPOSE

D EEP INSIDE, you know you have a greater destiny than the tribulations of your day to day life would seem to indicate.

T HIS is your soul purpose : the reason you are here, agreed by you before you came.

K NOWLEDGE of your purpose gives a focal point to your life : as you align your actions to the reason you are here you become more powerful, life more rewarding.

S O ASK YOURSELF : what is that great commitment hidden in your heart, the big achievement you secretly wish for but may never act upon?

THE charitable work you are drawn to : the world changing event for which you can be a catalyst?

THE wise support and counselling you can provide, which will serve to move others ahead?

THE creative gift you know lies dormant within, yet could benefit many?

THE action you dream of that would inspire thousands, yet from which you shrink?

SEEK guidance from within, be open with yourself and listen to your intuition : slowly, your soul purpose will emerge.

YOU will come to a position of clarity as to why you are here.

THEN, start to align your every action with what has been revealed.

FOR it is vital to your growth and happiness that you be true to your purpose : thereby you will find greater reward in living and make rapid progress.

SUCH self discovery empowers you : as a soul with a focus for action you can achieve all that you can visualise and are prepared to commit yourself to.

YOUR journey will be swift and sure.

CONNECTIONS

WE ARE NOT ALONE in our journey, for we have powerful connections in spirit.

OUR FIRST CONNECTION is earthly, for we are all linked by a global intelligence : we are each a part of it, and it is a part of us.

THERE are many examples that demonstrate humanity's inter-connection : -

THE EXCITEMENT of a football crowd ;

THE "HIGH" of a rock concert : the inspired precision of a great choir ;

THE RELIGIOUS ECSTACY of pilgrims as they pray ; the enthusiasm of a political rally ;

THE SHARED GRIEF we all feel at each new international disaster : for we unite in our sadness at suffering ;

STRANGE phenomena of the occult, mysticism, spirit manifestations and out-of-body experience.

OUR INDIVIDUAL SOULS also have many non-verbal communications : between auras, telepathic, on the astral and higher planes.

THESE ENERGY transactions are only beginning to be understood : they link us all in a human communications network.

THIS global intelligence is like a beehive where each small being is an individual : yet from outside the swarm is seen to act as one.

*F*OR WE ARE ONE in consciousness.

*T*HE SECOND CONNECTION is upward to the vast host of spirit beings that communicate to us from other dimensions : and through these connections, to universal intelligence, which many choose to call God.

*F*OR IT IS POSSIBLE to be directly in touch with other realms : they have a great deal of wisdom to give us if we choose to listen.

*A*ND THEY WISH to help by communicating advice and direction, when we request it.

*T*HE TECHNIQUES are simple and effective when approached in a spirit of exploration and humility.

*E*VEN TODAY you hear them as whispers and intuitions : this ability can be greatly enhanced.

*W*E have unimagined power through our soul and its interconnections : this power will steadily be released to you as you seek to open to inner wisdom.

*F*OR ALL HUMAN inspiration and creativity come from universal consciousness : by exploring and strengthening your spiritual links you enhance your power to create and make progress.

*T*HE EFFECT will change your perspective of yourself and your view and understanding of humanity for all time.

FINDING PEACE

IN ORDER TO make progress you must first be at peace with yourself.

LIVE YOUR LIFE in present time : there is no need to worry about things past, or what the future may hold : both merely diminish your attention on living.

THERE ARE WAYS of freeing yourself from the stress of past events and the worry of anticipated problems.

BY FOCUSSING yourself on the here and now, you increase the intensity of your life.

MAKE CLEAR commitments to yourself as to why you are here and what you wish to achieve in your life: then seek their attainment.

A CLEAR PURPOSE means that every action you take will be self empowering and in alignment with that purpose: your effectiveness in all that you do will be greatly increased.

BE AWARE of things spiritual: by developing your own spirituality you will benefit from the new perspectives that the materialistic amongst us can only reject.

IN ORDER TO MOVE forward give up confrontation and aggression: do not compare yourself jealously with others or indulge in bitter rivalries.

COMPETITION between people can assist self discovery and growth: but not when carried to extremes.

CONSTANT ARGUMENT with those to whom you are close is deeply damaging to your soul: work to cease rancour and live harmoniously.

INSTEAD OF creating or accepting constant pressure and acrimony around you, become open to new ways of being that provide better support for you and your loved ones.

AVOID THE company of loud and aggressive persons: they diminish your spirituality.

ESPECIALLY, do not hold a grudge against another or prosecute your case against them beyond its time : you cannot grow spiritually while filled with resentment.

WHILE it may well seem equitable to pursue those who have crossed you, be aware that the damage you do yourself will be greater than the impact on them.

RATHER, let the issue go and learn from it : the act will move your own growth forward.

BE wary of controlling others around you : for personal manipulation of others will one day be repaid in kind.

STRIVE INSTEAD to discover and become your real self, and reflect who you really are in your dealings with others: in so doing you will expand your power for good.

DEVELOP techniques of inspired debate and caring discussion in order to communicate new attitudes and possibilities, and carry others with you.

ENVY is also unnecessary: for you may be all you covet in another, and more. There are no limits to what you can achieve.

RELIGION

REMEMBER that all people are equal, despite colour, creed, wealth, culture or spiritual belief : treat them so. In truth they have the same status as you.

RESPECT those who embrace God through religion, whichever creed they follow : what they hold to be good is essentially true, even though their understanding may seem obscured by dogma.

BUT BE AWARE that much of religion has been diverted into forms of mass manipulation over many generations.

MANY religious messages in use today were intended for an earlier era : their meaning has been passed by. They now have little relevance.

VITAL and original wisdom that was intended for us all has long been buried by human theology.

WE WERE NOT ASKED by any great spiritual leader to raise up a priesthood in a hierarchy, and form a religion.

THE POWER TO CONTROL huge numbers of people is vested in religious structures : priests can thus assume greater importance than the message they bring.

YOU GIVE AWAY your power when you allow others to intercede on your behalf in this way.

RITUAL IN RELIGION has also assumed a false importance of its own : it serves only to distance us from the truth.

HUMANITY was wrong to have deified Christ as an omnipotent being : this served to distance him from us.

IT WAS ALWAYS his purpose to be accessible : to love us each individually.

BUT his teachings were diverted by organised religion : our fellow human beings made him remote and inaccessible as a means to control us.

CHRIST'S TEACHINGS are still of the greatest importance. He remains with us : concentrate on his message, and the example of his life.

*H*IS COMMITMENT is to take responsibility for the Earth and the progress of humanity.

*H*E IS A GREAT FRIEND, personal to you and not to be feared : our most important supporter in the spiritual realms. The Teachings of other great spiritual leaders have also been diverted from their true purpose, and used as instruments of mass control.

*T*HERE ARE MANY new religious sects emerging, and gathering energy : their powerful appeal will attract large numbers of people.

*T*HEIR HIGH LEVEL of commitment represents positive progress : they bring many new people to spirit.

*B*UT LOOK for pure intention and great integrity in such groups : manipulation and suppression of individuality remain a danger.

*B*E SELECTIVE in listening to those who preach : while it benefits you greatly to explore things spiritual, keep your critical faculties in place and be discerning.

*D*O NOT BE CONTENT to be a follower of others, but listen carefully to the words of those who offer spiritual guidance.

*H*AVE NO TIME for the manipulative cleric or religious zealot : their attitudes and teachings will not contribute to your spirituality.

*S*ELECT CAREFULLY that which you are prepared to embrace : invoke discernment and DEVELOP YOUR OWN TRUTH.

*F*OR if you merely follow others by rote, you too are open to manipulation.

*R*ATHER, trust your instinct. If you are true to yourself in matters of the spirit you will find that you are often right : then your progress will be rapid.

*C*HALLENGE what you hear from others in your own mind before accepting it.

FOR BELIEF is personal to each of us : its benefit is greatly reduced when controlled through a third party.

EACH of us has our own truth : we cannot succeed spiritually by forcing it on others or insisting that only our way is right.

PROPER spiritual guidance has value to many, but real progress comes only from inside.

ENJOY YOUR RELIGION, if you have one: but remember that your path to understanding is yours alone.

RECOGNISE that there are many who believe deeply in the spiritual while rejecting formal religion : they, too, are moving forward in their journey. Perhaps they have the advantage.

EXPLORE YOUR IDEAS and experiences with others, especially those of different persuasions: you will find many who will understand and support you, giving mutual strength, energy and love.

FINDING OR FORMING a group of like-minded people will give you joy : and enhance your growth as you explore.

IN SUCH A GROUP, commit to mutuality and unconditional love : you will find it both safe and fun to experience the group energy.

THEIR ENERGY in support of you greatly increases your spiritual power : yet be aware that the primary beneficiary of loving support is the one who gives it.

IN ORDER TO GAIN a truer perspective on our daily life, set aside a little time each day to cut out the clamour of the world outside.

LEARN TO MEDITATE daily : it aids the recovery and focussing of your spirit and helps you transcend daily pressures. By so doing your growth will accelerate.

PRAYER provides communication with higher planes : it gives you great practical power.

L EARN TO USE PRAYER *and meditation, and your world will shift to help you.*

I N ASKING FOR SUPPORT, *expect solutions to be offered : be both positive and prepared to act.*

37

K A R M A

IN EVERY LIFE we spend here we build up credits and debits : the system is called Karma.

OUR task through many lives is to experience and grow : and thus to achieve balance in our being.

AS we move forward our spiritual energies increase in frequency, and our sensitivity in the higher realms becomes greater.

EVERY ACTION we take, in every life, is recorded and will be played back in some form, so that our misalignments can be balanced.

KARMA is created when our thoughts and actions are out of alignment with our purpose and those around us : we are then held back until the debt is repaid.

ONLY when this process is complete can we graduate to the next level : restitution is obtained by reversal of our experience.

THE TERRORIST will have his lesson in being terrorised.

THE RELIGIOUS BIGOT will experience great intolerance.

THE RAPIST will be forced into total vulnerability.

THOSE who have practiced violence will be violated.

THE ONE who holds hatred for other races will reincarnate into that tribe which was most despised.

BIBLICAL WRITINGS once gave detailed instruction to humanity on Reincarnation and the laws of Karma.

THIS VITAL WISDOM was removed by a powerfully misaligned human being who sought to deny future retribution for great wrong doing.

THIS KNOWLEDGE has survived as basic understanding, the foundation to other religions : and, unrecognised, in our everyday speech.

FAMILIAR SAYINGS refer to the laws of Karma : Do as you would be done by, As ye sow, so shall ye reap.

AN EYE FOR AN EYE, a tooth for a tooth . This is not an encouragement for revenge : it is a warning that the giver of these deeds will be revisited as recipient.

IN THIS TIME of new energies from the cosmos, those who are of the light can now process Karma more rapidly than before.

SIMPLE ACTIONS of acknowledgement can exorcise great misdeeds in former lives, and allow us to move on : we are thus forgiven for past action.

THERE IS ALSO great credit to be won : the giving and receiving of love generates positive energies that support our progress.

EVERY POSITIVE thought or deed is accounted to our credit : such action also draws positive people and events to us.

A LOVING way of being is thus self-reinforcing.

BUT the laws of Karma still apply to our present actions : the consequences of misaligned action in this time of the light will be found in judgement.

THOSE who do not seek harmony will be given every opportunity to change : if they fail to act they will eventually fall back to the lowest level.

FOR THEM the course work in this school called Earth will be repeated through many more lives.

SPIRITUAL PROGRESS

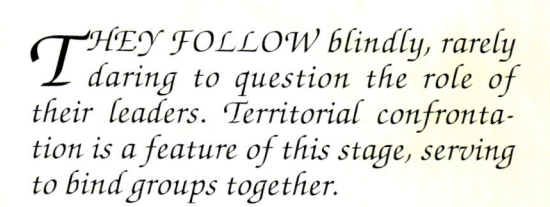

OUR OBJECT IN developing through our many lives on Earth is to reach the highest level of spiritual consciousness, while being physically fulfilled.

IT TAKES MANY such experiences to master this art of being human.

THERE ARE SEVEN LEVELS of human spirituality that we all go through : each has its sub-levels.

THE FIRST IS TRIBAL : its conscious concern is with survival, to find food and shelter, to sleep and reproduce.

THE NEXT is feudal : geographical groupings of people are organised by the strongest warriors, to whom they give fealty.

THEY FOLLOW blindly, rarely daring to question the role of their leaders. Territorial confrontation is a feature of this stage, serving to bind groups together.

LEVEL THREE is the emergence of the individual : ego develops, personal ambition appears and thinking becomes centred around the self.

THESE ARE THE teenage years of spirituality : many are fast climbers who step on all around them to advance material position and status.

THE FOURTH LEVEL is the aspirant, an individual who has realised that some greater power is a fact of life : that 'God is out there, somewhere'.

THIS REALISATION will often express itself in a commitment to religion.

AS FOCUS IS ACHIEVED in seeking and understanding the basics of spirituality, the disciple emerges.

IN THIS, THE FIFTH LEVEL, an alternative understanding of God and the universe begins to develop.

A GURU may be followed. Philosophy emerges as a component of spiritual thinking: a monastic or hermitic element enters the individual's way of being.

THIS STAGE is about following others in search of an answer: there will be many blind alleys and wrong turnings.

PAINFUL EXPERIENCE guides the spiritual warrior through many such lessons.

THE BATTLE-SCARRED warrior will eventually learn that truth comes only from within: he can then move on.

AT THE SIXTH LEVEL the guru is finally abandoned, and the initiate emerges.

THE INITIATE comes to an understanding of karmic responsibility : knowing that one is held accountable for every action in every life, be it positive or negative.

THE ACCOUNTABILITY is cumulative: many souls are thus burdened by karmic debt from actions taken earlier in their spiritual journey.

THE TASK OF THE initiate is to balance karmic debt by internal growth and personal healing : positive action that benefits others allows such debt to be repaid.

THIS LEADS to the seventh, and final, level of spirituality: mastery of the art of being fully human.

MASTERY IS ACHIEVED when all the lessons are learnt and karmic balance is struck.

THIS LEVEL IS dedicated, above all, to serving the world and its population: even to the sacrifice of self in supporting others on their spiritual journey.

THE MASTER may become the guru for others, but never seeks this role.

PHYSICAL CHANGE accompanies this spiritual development : it is driven by our change in energies.

IF WE VIEW our physical world at the atomic level, we discover that it consists of many levels of energy vibration: the same is true of spiritual energy, but at a higher frequency.

AT EACH NEW LEVEL of consciousness we gain spiritual energy: our power increases, and with it the level of vibration of our physical and spiritual being.

TOTAL MASTERY reaches a level of enlightenment fully connected with universal consciousness: high spiritual vibration allows the master to ascend into the spirit world at will.

THE ASCENDED MASTER moves between the spiritual and the physical with ease: the perfect combination of body and spirit.

ONLY A FEW have ascended so far: but Ascension is the grand design for all of us.

THEY WHO HAVE gone before us have chosen to spend further time on earth in human form during the transition: they are here to help us.

FOR OUR PHYSICAL world is to become a paradise.

INTUITION & CREATIVITY

*I*NTUITION is the voice of your soul: its use is a key step in your fulfilment.

*T*HE UNIVERSE holds the answers that you seek: with care and attention to your intuitive connections you will receive valuable guidance.

*B*UT FIRST, you must learn how to listen.

*F*IND QUIET TIME and space to focus inwardly and encourage your intuition to work.

*D*ISCOVER THE PLACE that works for you: inspiring buildings, open spaces, the night sky.

*T*HE SOLITUDE of the forest or proximity to water.

A QUIET SPACE in your own home: any environment which causes your spirit to stir and your consciousness to soar will support you.

*E*VEN IF you have no religion, you may find that places of worship have the calmness and solitude you require.

A GREAT CHURCH SPIRE is like a lightening conductor for your spiritual connections: a dome is like a vessel to collect and store spiritual energy.

*S*TAND under them quietly and you will feel your spirituality soar.

*L*ISTEN ATTENTIVELY for guidance, for your most valuable thoughts may be fleeting: intuition is quicker and more powerful than processes of logic, so you must be attuned.

*L*EARN TO HEAR such guidance accurately and develop the confidence to follow its direction: properly understood it will enhance all aspects of your life.

*B*E CONSTANTLY alert and test every intuitive message: try to be sure that it is not just the product of ego.

*T*HEN you can act on what you have received.

*F*OR YOU HAVE a purpose here: intuition leads you to harmony with that purpose. Little will then stand in your way.

INTUITION is closely linked with creativity : both require an openness of mind and willingness to step outside established habit. They are mutually reinforcing.

A COMBINATION of great creativity and spirituality allows you to manifest the things that you want in life : for these spiritual tools give us the power to change our reality.

YOU can create new realities : the ability is yours to use when you accept responsibility for all that happens in your life.

IT is our judgemental nature and the programming of experience that works against creativity and spiritual understanding : they negate completely our power to manifest.

WE NEED TO programme new mental faculties for positive and constructive ways of thinking.

FIRST, DISTINGUISH between ways of thinking that are precise and rigid and those which are soft and exploratory.

THE FORMER are for clearly defined tasks : but the latter are far more conducive of creativity and encourage intuition.

AN ABLE MIND can be trained to call on either approach at will.

THEN, CHALLENGE your habit of judgement.

WE ARE conditioned to see every issue in terms of right and wrong : little or nothing that passes goes unjudged by us.

WE THROW OUT much that is valuable in the process: another approach is needed if we are to enhance our learning ability.

THEREFORE, build a new space in your mind for that which is a possibility : in it place and keep those claims and ideas which are neither proven nor disproven.

FOR MANY STRANGE phenomena have no good explanation and some new ideas may at first seem crazy : yet you cannot profit from them if they are thrown out at the first opportunity.

POSSIBILITY consciousness results from making this new space : an addition to your thinking faculties which will help you grow in creativity and understanding.

FOR MOST of us this provides a new way of viewing our experiences : it opens options for progress that were not previously visible.

WHEN YOU HOLD many unproven things to be a possibility, some will start to merge into each other, and reveal new levels of understanding.

INCREASED consciousness enhances all those powers that are based in spirit.

CREATIVITY ALSO brings to many the benefits of enjoyment, inspiration, and employment: and to each of you who chooses to be Creator, the delight of working with higher energies.

THUS our creativity brings power and imagination into play to generate abundance in its broadest sense, and the satisfaction of understanding.

AS WE DEVELOP our powers, and the connections that go with them, we move closer to the metamorphosis that will fulfil the human design.

HEALTH & BODY

YOU ARE a being of light : your soul is pure energy and is indestructible.

YOUR BODY is a space suit rented for your present incarnation : you occupy it until it can no longer support your soul, or you are ready to leave.

HONOUR YOUR physical self, for the condition of your body will aid your spiritual being. In turn, your view of yourself will benefit your long term health : and your longevity.

THERE ARE MANY WAYS to increase the life span, but the body is a physical system : with humanity's present way of being, it will eventually fail.

YET DEATH as we know it will eventually become unnecessary : leaving this world a matter of choice and not of physical decay.

FOR HUMANITY is meant to live in a constant state of wellness, and is equipped to do so.

SO, SET ASIDE some time for physical activity and keep your body efficient : it will then last longer and work more effectively as your soul's environment for this incarnation.

YOUR BODY contains powerful systems which are energised by the way you breathe and by what you eat and drink.

BODY ENERGIES extend well outside your physical body. They can be seen and felt with a little training : even photographed with the right equipment.

THE AURA and chakras are parts of these body energy systems.

AN EXPERT in body energy can detect blockages in the systems that will develop into illness if unattended : and has the skills to heal them.

DIET is a vital element in spiritual growth, and can enhance your ability to focus on higher planes.

BREATHING SYSTEMS have been devised which increase both body and spiritual energy : in so doing they expand your consciousness.

MANY ALTERNATIVE forms of healing have been developed around the world : they are now being adopted from many different cultures, and their use is spreading.

THE BEST ARE HOLISTIC in approach, dealing with mind, body and soul as one complete entity.

THEY COME from a higher understanding of how we are designed : often they are seen to challenge conventional medicine, when they should complement and extend it.

FOR THE MEDICAL world is riddled with dogma and professional jealousies.

PROFESSIONAL politics seek to prevent alternative healing techniques from being widely applied : but acceptance of them steadily grows without regard.

TAKE A HOLISTIC VIEW of the state of your own body : every emotion you experience or action you take has its physical side effects.

LONG TERM emotional stress or unresolved pressure from the way we conduct our lives over many years sow the seeds for physical illness : death is thus an accumulated effect.

SO BE KIND to yourself in the conduct of your life : many stresses will be relieved and both your body and soul will benefit accordingly.

WITHOUT being obsessive be aware of your eating habits and follow an appropriate diet.

DRUGS, ALCOHOL and fatty foods taken to excess will soon take their toll : be moderate in their use.

AS YOUR SPIRITUALITY progresses, you will automatically move to refine your diet : higher spirit energy will lead to a lightening of body tissue and will change the nourishment you need.

YOUR BODY will become increasingly efficient in absorbing energy, and therefore require less of it.

THERE IS GOOD NEWS in personal health : at the highest level of spirituality, the physical body becomes self healing. Humanity is moving in this direction.

LIFE EXPECTANCY is rapidly increasing in the more affluent parts of the world : concern for fitness, good dietary practices and the advancing of medical technology is extending our lives.

WE HAVE THE CAPACITY to cure disabling disease and to regenerate considerable physical damage.

THE DEGREE to which self healing can be achieved depends on spiritual maturity, balance and ability to focus positively on the causes of the problem.

BUT REMEMBER that effect comes only after cause : repair and recovery is difficult if the illness has been caused by many years of abuse in living.

THEREFORE, new medical technologies are important for many who have treatable ailments : for them the spiritual remedy is too late. Physical treatment is the way ahead.

WHATEVER METHOD is chosen, a strong spiritual base will provide support in enhancing physical healing.

SO DO NOT DENY the benefits of medical advance for the sake of strong convictions or religious dogma : they are here for our benefit.

MANY TECHNOLOGIES will be introduced : regeneration techniques for limbs and organs will become commonplace. We will use genetic engineering to eliminate inherited disorders.

IT IS NATURAL that the introduction of such methods will cause controversy and disquiet : yet do not resist merely out of reactionary feeling.

RATHER, THINK about them and their contribution to humanity : accept new ways if they are soundly based in wider morality, for they may have real benefit.

BE DISCERNING : for, properly used, these advances are a valuable gift.

D Y I N G

YOU have no need to be afraid of death : you existed before you came here, and you will continue to exist after you leave.

YOU SET your objectives for this life before you came.

YOU WILL TRY to see that they are met before you die : for no-one leaves this Earth until they are quite ready.

BEING HERE ON EARTH is a process of learning : you have been here many times before, have encountered many lessons, and have grown at every stage.

THUS you have experienced death before.

THE ACT OF DYING at the end of this life will be a great relief to you and is perfectly safe : you will go home to rest and review what you have achieved.

YOU MAY THEN ELECT to come to Earth again if more needs to be learnt.

SO, when a loved one leaves you, do not grieve for long : they have moved to a place of release and enlightenment.

RATHER, CELEBRATE the elevation of your friend to a higher plane : and their escape from the trials of the physical to a place of renewal, returning to incarnation only when they are ready.

WE were not intended to be captives of the physical world, but to develop at a more spiritual level : to become a perfect combination of physical and spiritual, with great powers to create.

BUT THE MASTER PLAN went astray.

IN ANCIENT times we were diverted from our intended path of growth and development : misaligned spirit beings were the cause of the breakdown.

OUR LOSS OF DIRECTION caused our separation from the God who had always been our intimate : thus evolved humanity's great insecurity within.

THE STORY of the Garden of Eden illustrates our premature gaining of knowledge. We were diverted from our path and our journey became difficult.

LOSS OF CONTACT with God and the spirit world has been a great constraint and source of conflict : a spiritual millstone that has made death appear a finality.

YET IT IS NOT SO, for our souls transcend the physical body.

DEATH IS MERELY release from the physical burden : allowing you to meet once again with those who haved moved on.

AFTER REST AND REVIEW you may once again elect to return to Earth.

THROUGH THE LESSONS of many individual lives humanity is slowly returning to its proper path, after eons of being lost in Earth's physical wilderness.

FEAR, EGO & EMOTION

SEEK to embrace the changes that begin to happen around you : but also be properly cautious.

DO NOT GIVE WAY to fear : it is a prime root of evil. It brings spiritual stagnation, a halt to growth.

FEAR INHIBITS YOU from positive action : resist its power over you or your progress will be lost.

FEAR can be real and appropriate: when an accident or physical attack is imminent, do not ponder the evidence, but act quickly.

BUT MANY FEARS exist only in the mind, with the imagination anticipating and exaggerating the worst of what may happen.

DISTINGUISH CLEARLY between real and imaginary fear, for the latter is disabling of body and spirit.

SUCH FEAR must be exorcised if you are to make progress : by living in present time you will do much to diminish its effect.

FOR SOME whose fears dominate their lives, support and counselling will provide a framework for resolution.

THERE is no stigma in seeking such help where needed : your life will improve as a result.

YOUR MOST PERSONAL FEARS, whatever they may be, cause suffering to those you love : be aware that insecurity can destroy your most valued relationships.

ALSO, DO NOT MAKE others fear you : you have enough to do in this life without making enemies.

YOUR EGO is a powerful tool which helps you define who you are and how you relate to others in this physical world : it is also dangerous and destructive if allowed to dominate.

EGO is yours to control : use it positively and learn to switch it off when it is not needed. This ability is an advantage in daily life, especially when negotiating with others.

LOOK FOR WAYS to neutralise your fears and use your ego positively.

*E*MOTION is a physical sensa-tion to which you have attached a powerful thought that in turn can dominate your whole being : you can be a hostage to emotion, and thus lose much progress.

*W*HEN YOUR EMOTIONS are in danger of controlling you, seek to reduce them to the feelings in your body : by this means you can help yourself to regain control.

*B*Y loving the feelings exactly as you experience them, emotion is integrated and negative effects are nullified.

*Y*ET TAKE CARE not to deny emotion, for it is a part of your humanity : simply do not let it take you over.

*F*EAR, ego and emotion are tools of your being : used well they help your growth and the expres-sion of your purpose.

*C*ONDUCT YOURSELF with gentleness, openness and confidence, with emotional aware-ness, and friendship will blossom around you. Yet be firm and decisive when appropriate.

55

LOVE

LOVE IS LOVE : the universe is based upon it. It is the creative energy of the universe, and has many forms.

THE LOVE YOU show yourself is the deciding factor in the love you can give to others.

FIRST YOU MUST learn to love yourself : you are a creature of great complexity and potential.

YOU ARE MAGNIFICENT : so take time to appreciate who and what you are. Hold in awe the fact of your own being.

GIVEN proper love of yourself you can then love any person, group or life form : the possibilities are unlimited.

THE GIVING OF LOVE is present in all our relationships : be it with a friend, colleague, relative or any of those about you, love is the same quality.

YOU CANNOT love selectively : in a perfect situation you merely experience love differently with each individual in your life.

TO CONSTRAIN ANOTHER by demanding exclusivity in love is thus to diminish them by constraining their options : if you succeed they simply cease to grow.

THE LOVE YOU SHARE with a lover is the same love that you give to others but your experience is magnified by the energies arising from intimacy of both soul and body.

WHEN YOU MAKE physical love, you bring in the creative energies from the universe : it is a supreme energy transaction between you.

THE LOVE YOU GIVE children and family is also powerful and provides the security of bonding.

COMMIT TO VALUE your loving relationships above events that may affect them : to preserve love and not let relationships be undermined by rules or circumstances.

UNCONDITIONAL LOVE has no rules, the giver no expectations : simply love the others you choose to be with for who they are, separate from any consideration as to what they may do as they progress through life.

BY HAVING no conditions to the love you give, you cannot be hurt : you have no expectation to disappoint you.

SEEK TO LOVE at the soul level, without terms : you then create a relationship that will extend beyond this lifetime.

PURE, UNCONDITIONAL love is the perfect form of communication.

THE LOVE of the universe and between those beings at spiritual levels above us is unconditional and eternal : it is the way of higher beings and the direction in which humanity is evolving.

IF YOU IMPOSE impossible rules and conditions on how you are prepared to love another you store up pain for yourself : when a partner steps outside the terms you seek to impose, you will feel great anguish.

BY LOVING conditionally, your love will eventually be turned to hatred or self-deception : your imposed conditions will be self defeating.

THE ONLY VALID and lasting commitment we make is to love unconditionally, without consideration or concern as to what may happen in the future.

LOVING without conditions is not easy : it requires you to accept that those you love are human, and will inevitably make mistakes.

INTIMATE RELATIONSHIPS

EVERY RELATIONSHIP has its paradigm : a blueprint for each individual's thoughts and feelings about the other.

YOUR PERSONAL paradigms condition how you interact with others : it is all too easy to adopt paradigms that serve only to ensure loneliness.

WORK TO CREATE a small circle of close friends, and conduct yourself so as not to be constantly lonely. The opposite of loneliness is intimacy, which supports your spiritual growth.

FRIENDSHIP is truly respecting each other : intimacy is thus friendship carried to a point of complete trust and unconditional love.

UNDERSTANDING your own requirements for a relationship well and communicating them clearly to those you love makes possible a successful paradigm for intimacy : and the entering of long-term partnerships.

IF YOU HAVE A LOVER, make no assumptions about where you expect the relationship to lead, without mutual agreement : share your thoughts and yet be clear that you cannot enforce agreement to them.

ABOVE ALL, be flexible with your partner : having understood each others' wishes, remember that neither of you is perfect in the execution of what you intend.

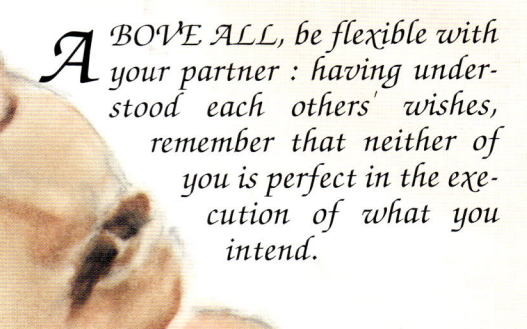

YOU CANNOT OWN your partner in a relationship, neither is your partner a personal territory to be guarded : do not seek to control and manipulate those whom you love.

PHYSICAL SEXUALITY is an extension of love and can be an exclusive arrangement by agreement: enjoy your closeness, and work mutually to generate each others' pleasure.

A COMMITTED and exclusive relationship can be joyful : it is a good idea to have a written contract between you. It should be examined and agreed, clause by clause, between you.

YOU ARE THEN more likely to understand the commitments you make.

MARRIAGE is a relationship perpetuated with formal expectations and the signing of papers : but you cannot relax in security after your vows are made, and expect the fact of marriage to guard your relationship.

TO avoid failure, work together to improve what you have : build a common purpose to which you are both committed and your relationship will be strengthened.

TREASURE your partner's love for you and do not abuse it because of your jealousy of others.

HOLD in your mind that if your partner truly loves you, any relationship they have with another does not threaten you : jealousy will always damage you and never enhances the relationship you have.

WITH MUTUAL agreement and caring you may even find fulfilment with more than one partner but only in the context of love and not one of greed.

BE OPEN about such arrangements : you are very fortunate if your partners understand and continue to love you.

YOU will find no joy in continual promiscuity, which also has its physical dangers: only unsatisfactory partnership or innate insecurity will force you to deceive with short-term sexual liaisons. Touching is important: a warm hug is a true expression of closeness and caring.

TENDERNESS with your partner is not only a pleasure to you both : it is also a great preserver and will help you overcome many difficulties.

IN YOUR LOVEMAKING, make a mutual agreement with your partner that your purpose is the other's pleasure and satisfaction : you will thus receive a great gift from each other.

P A R T I N G

A RELATIONSHIP is like a bank balance for the emotions : give and take on an equal basis with your partner and all should be well.

B UT if you are hopelessly over-drawn your partner must eventually foreclose.

G IVE a new partnership enough time to mature : but should your expectations turn out to be far apart, it is fair to walk away.

I F A RELATIONSHIP gives you constant pain, all reconciliation has failed and little pleasure remains, let it go.

M UCH ANGUISH will arise from trying to change the ways of a partner who does not share your objectives : energy spent trying to revive the irrevivable is wasted.

F OR in some relationships the partners have simply given all that they have to offer.

B OTH have benefitted from their time together : but personal growth has ceased and the pressures of a fast-moving world have taken them in different directions.

I T MAY THEN be time that the arrangement between you should end : if so, conduct yourself with love for the other person, and appreciation of what they have contributed to you.

W ITH a little consideration you can both withdraw with dignity and in friendship : there is no need for your self regard to be in ruins.

O PEN DISCUSSION between you is the key.

T HINK WELL of those who you have loved in the past : if they were as bad as you may now imagine, how do you rate your own wisdom in so choosing?

D O NOT CARRY bitterness or regret : rather, think of the good things you shared and your growth together, and not of the pain of parting.

$\mathcal{B}$E READY to celebrate the positive aspects of the relationship you are leaving.

$\mathcal{A}$LWAYS ALLOW yourself to greet a past lover with discreet warmth and affection : if you are both honest with yourselves you will see that it represents a truth between you. It will be appreciated by the other.

$\mathcal{G}$REAT FRIENDSHIPS can blossom between past lovers : once you have shared such a close relationship, potential exists for respect and mutual understanding.

$\mathcal{V}$ALUE CONTINUING FRIENDSHIP, and do not break away in bitterness, for true relationships are not confined to the physical : and they last beyond this life and temporal circumstance.

$\mathcal{I}$F YOU HAVE been badly hurt by the failure of past relationships it is not necessary or healthy to withdraw into loneliness or celibacy for long.

$\mathcal{I}$SOLATION or promiscuity are frequent reactions to a failed relationship : work hard to overcome either, for they represent a slide into spiritual negativity.

$\mathcal{D}$EVISE a personal recovery plan : for it is beneficial to return to intimacy in a good partnership.

$\mathcal{F}$IRST, allow a little while for healing : take time to recover your confidence and re-align your attitudes.

$\mathcal{B}$EFORE you try again, adjust your paradigm : value your aloneness and learn to be comfortable with it.

$\mathcal{S}$EEK NEW FRIENDS, develop new interests and actively expand yourself : in choosing a new partner, be sure that your choice is not driven merely by loneliness.

$\mathcal{W}$HEN YOU ARE READY, seek another with whom you are closer to agreement.

$\mathcal{D}$ISCUSS AND AGREE a fair set of assumptions and expectations : take time to ensure the relationship is well founded.

$\mathcal{A}$CT with balance and avoid hasty choices : in so doing your chance of being hurt again is greatly diminished.

CHILDREN

OUR CHILDREN are not ours to keep : they are merely lent to us for a few short years.

THEY ARE SENT to teach us : many an old soul now lives in a young body.

THE CHILD YOU LOVE has been here many times : perhaps as someone close in one of your previous lives.

THINK OF THE CHILDREN you know and love : ponder where they may have been, and what they may have done when they were here before.

HONOUR EACH CHILD for the possibility of who they really are.

CHILDREN have a simplicity of vision we can all benefit from : they see the world around them with awe and wonder. Their perspective is not yet jaded.

IN EARLY YOUTH they have not been conditioned to suppress their natural wisdom : intuition is high and understanding uncluttered.

EXPLORATION and growth are their natural way of being : they delight in discovery and their perfect insight carries them forward.

THEY BELIEVE that every-thing is possible and show limit-less imagination : they can see things of the spirit that we cannot.

THEY HAVE natural trust and unconditional love for all around them : in their early years, we have yet to teach them otherwise.

FOR LIFE is only beginning to demonstrate its constraints, and their elders to impose their bound-aries on youthful thinking.

WHEN you talk to children treat them as equals from an early age : you will be surprised by the consistent maturity and directness of their response.

THEIR WORDS are valuable if you are prepared to treat them seriously: they have many messages that are specific to you.

LISTEN CAREFULLY to what they say : they speak wisdom that is uncluttered and without reticence.

A TRUTH AS SPOKEN by a child will often be too painful for you to hear and readily accept : directness that causes you discomfort is a clear sign of a message you need to receive.

TRY TO GO BACK in time to the way you used to see the World : if you can view the World as a child does, you will gain greatly in spiritu-ality and throw off many of today's burdens.

WHEN YOUR CHILDREN are ready to leave, you must be willing to let them go and help them on their way : they are souls on a jour-ney, just as you are.

YOU CANNOT constrain them beyond their time with you, for they, too, must move forward, and may eventually outrun us.

HUMANITY is rapidly evolving : we see the changes first in new powers given to our children.

EACH NEW GENERATION is changing the definition of humanity : previously unexplored fac-ulties of mind and spirit are becoming more developed in each new human child.

CAUSES

THERE are many causes in the world that are worthy of support : there are many who need help.

IT IS A SIGN of our humanity to experience pain when we see the suffering of others : yet we are not personally responsible for their plight.

THE VICTIMS feel no such emotion, and do not seek to hold us to account.

SUCH FEELINGS merely get in the way of practical help and are inappropriate : yet do not hesitate to commit yourself to a specific cause, after proper consideration.

THE greatest contribution to your own spiritual growth is to serve others. Do so with humility and keep a low profile : true service is not an act of self publicity.

YOU can serve at three different levels : an understanding of your options is thus important.

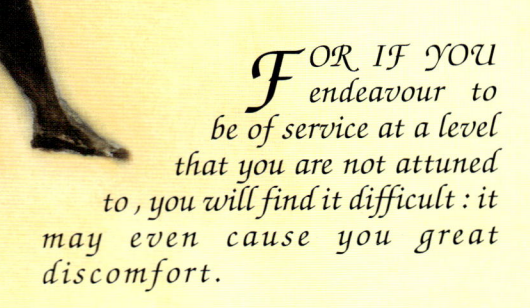

FOR IF YOU endeavour to be of service at a level that you are not attuned to, you will find it difficult : it may even cause you great discomfort.

THE FIRST OPTION is to serve individuals : by encouraging and helping those immediately around you to live and grow successfully within their own environment.

THE SECOND is to work for the society in which you live : by public service, or by campaigning to improve national or local rules and changing the framework in which people operate.

THE THIRD is to work for humanity : to help bring about those shifts in consciousness and changes in focus that give effect to global change.

THINK CAREFULLY as to which level best suits your ability and interests : follow your intuition, and be assured that all service is of great value, regardless of the level at which it is given.

IF YOU THEN WISH to support a cause, at any level, make an active choice as to which it should be.

SOME CAUSES are in the form of organised charities : some may be personal to you. Set out those that you wish to consider.

TRY to understand their real needs and gain insight into the actions required for progress in the work that they do.

SEE how alternatives you may consider fit the realities of life : ask yourself each cause's real value to the world.

SATISFY YOURSELF that each organisation is real and effective : for there are charities whose true reasons for being are deeply suspect or whose finances are diverted from their stated purpose.

*B*E CLEAR in your heart that those who operate the organisation have integrity : that they have both the ability and intention to deliver what they promise.

*C*HARITABLE organisations may become a power base for one or more individuals : their focus is often in the politics of the organisation, not in giving service.

*S*UCH ACTIVITY is out of alignment with real needs : the protagonists become set in their ways, resistant to necessary change if it threatens their power base.

*O*FTEN, they impose solutions on those they claim to help, their activity resented by the recipients.

*A*VOID organisations that are riddled with politics, and have little sensitivity : your purpose is not to gratify the manipulative.

*T*HERE are also organisations who endorse extreme action in pursuit of the cause they promote.

*T*HERE is no cause that justifies violence : those who act to terrorise merely complicate the situation they purport to help. They violate their own souls in the process.

*T*HE PENALTY for violent action in any cause is to go backwards in spiritual growth : ensuring many lives on Earth , making reparations for negative karma.

*S*O BE DISCERNING about who you support : do not give comfort to those who are not of good intent, or are politically manipulative, or who practice violence in the name of good works.

*R*EVIEW each of your causes with care.

*T*HEN choose a principal cause to support and concentrate on it : know why you give your support, and be clear what commitment you are prepared to make.

*E*FFECTIVENESS in serving comes from focus : not from disipating yourself in many directions.

*R*EMEMBER that you cannot carry the burdens of the whole world.

*D*O NOT TRY to support every worthy cause, or worry about every world issue : in so doing you will only disable yourself.

*R*ATHER be clear when you elect to take responsibility to help others.

GOVERNMENT AID

*I*N a vigorous and expanding world there have always been those who are poor or sick or otherwise disadvantaged.

*M*ANY problems of food, health and personal safety have assumed Global proportions.

*I*NDIVIDUALS are the catalyst for help : but large organisations and governments are needed to support and enable effective action on a global scale.

*Y*ET governments can never do enough to eliminate these problems.

*F*INANCIAL support to disadvantaged people must be given with care : it may soon be seen as a right and can then cause great resentment.

*M*ANY individuals who have failed to take responsibility for themselves automatically take improper advantage if the state uses support funds badly.

*W*ELL-MEANING handouts often serve to extinguish incentive where more appropriate support would encourage self sufficiency.

*G*RANT AID given by wealthy governments to developing countries can generate greed and dishonesty by intermediaries : often, it will not get to those who are in need.

*F*AR better to provide a framework for self help : provision of the necessary tools and methods to encourage self reliance is the most effective way.

*A*ID agencies must proceed with sensitivity : it is not necessary to sacrifice cultures when giving aid and support.

*S*UCH gifts require a clearer understanding of real needs by the donor : a personal commitment to achievement by those who are being helped.

*G*IVEN opportunity, proper support and encouragement, even the poorest will begin to create their own wealth.

*T*HE answers to poverty, hunger, sickness and war lie in strategic change : only new global strategies can remove these problems at source.

*T*HE SOLUTIONS will become easier as peoples are honoured for their differences, and we abandon the pressure for industrial and cultural uniformity.

*O*NLY then will we care sufficiently to end global deprivation once and for all.

WORLD FINANCE

THE WORLD'S real wealth and its medium of interchange have long been divorced from each other.

INCREASINGLY, money, credit and financial instruments no longer represent reality : they are a contrived fiction of a few powerful bodies.

LARGE TRACTS of the Earth's real wealth have been hijacked by centuries of exploitation.

FOR every trade transaction across national boundaries there are ten which are speculation in currency or commodities.

THIS FOCUS on speculation is a global obsession. It leads only to instability : it does not serve the common good.

THE continuous drive for constant economic growth is an aberration based on institutionalised greed : it cannot be sustained.

CURRENT financial regimes will not last in their present form : the largest national economies of the World are technically bankrupt.

A MAJOR financial crisis is only held off by the complexity of international finance systems : and the conspiring together of those who run them.

NEW global perspectives on protection of resources, and increasing instability of existing financial systems will soon lead to radical change.

TODAY'S SYSTEMS will be replaced by a value standard based on energy, physical and human resources and tangible values : and thus on reality.

SUCH a standard brings the opportunity for a single world currency which is grounded in resources : and naturally inflation proof.

FOR NOW, there is a great power struggle for financial supremacy : whereas banks once held the cash deposits of the world, these have been steadily taken over by other institutions.

THE pension funds and the insurance companies control ever greater proportions of the world's wealth.

BOTH bank control and liquidity have been irrevocably weakened in the process.

A STEADY REDUCTION in the number of currencies will reduce the complexity of International transactions : and with it the opportunity to speculate, and many associated banking functions.

THIS PROCESS is the fore-runner of even greater change.

T A X A T I O N

THOSE WHO GOVERN are here to serve the people : yet they forget their true role with consummate ease.

THEIR ABILITY to levy taxes tempts them to seek ever greater expansion and control.

THERE are proper duties and functions for government to perform : it is right that these should be paid for.

BUT continual expansion means that much individual wealth is confiscated to support unjustified overheads.

SUCH confiscation cannot work positively for long.

GOVERNMENTS have invented many taxes over the years : their organisations have created an insatiable demand for funding.

THE PROCEEDS of taxation should further the common good without reducing human initiative.

THERE are support services that are needed, but many activities supported by government are misplaced or hopelessly inefficient.

WHEN USED merely to create secure but purposeless employment or to build great power bases, taxation is simply a form of theft.

MANY FUNCTIONS of government have now become unnecessary : there is great potential for tax burdens to be decreased.

MILITARY competition and bureaucratic barriers to trade are becoming redundant.

SMALL COMPUTERS serve to eliminate the need for many layers of administration : and thus save costs.

MANY PUBLIC SERVICES can be carried out more effectively, and at less cost, by non-government bodies.

SOME OF THE WORK undertaken by individual governments are of a global nature and are better co-ordinated by global institutions.

GOVERNMENT and people often confuse equality of opportunity with legislated equality : the former is a fine ideal, the latter, misguided and destructive.

ENFORCED EQUALITY is like a convoy : all are constrained to move at the speed of the slowest.

CONCEPTS of common ownership may set an interesting example to others when people live communally : but only as a chosen way of living.

WHEN THE STATE seeks to dominate ownership and regulate opportunity and living standards by legislation or force, they follow unworkable dogma.

IT IS NOT for government to redistribute wealth.

ATTEMPTS TO DO SO lead to the worst abuses of freedom : they disable those who create wealth and employment. In the long term society becomes poorer.

TAKE CARE not to thrust your own responsibilities on to your government : in such an attitude lies the seeds of growing governmental control.

BY SO DOING you give away your power : you are personally diminished in the process.

WAR & POLITICS

WE HUMAN BEINGS look for leadership in times of trouble : leadership which becomes an assumed control.

IN FEUDAL TIMES power was vested in the local Lord or Squire : the struggle was between adjacent districts. From such struggle, nations emerged.

PRESSURE and problems over territory, rights and scarce resources have always ensured the continuance of the tribe : it has been a prime reason for nationhood.

FOR THE WESTERN nations the last two centuries have been about struggle to control world resources : for the domination of global trade and territory.

MUCH OF THE WORLD is still essentially feudal, yet modern communications have created a global desire for change.

DEVELOPING nations now seek to compress into a single generation that which took others hundreds of years.

IN SOME COUNTRIES, demands for fair treatment, democracy and freedom of speech lead to military action : now presented to the world through the medium of television.

WHAT WE SEE is often a brutal lesson to the developed world, causing seed change in understanding and attitudes : for there is always resistance to such change.

YET those countries that offend merely follow the earlier example of other nations.

FOR GOVERNMENTS of all forms, motivated by greed for power and territory, have long manipulated their people to believe in what they choose to call the National Interest.

NATIONALISM leads to great and violent excess : as a builder of barriers between peoples, it does not serve humanity.

*S*UCH IDEOLOGY supports the politician's tenure, so creating false public issues that must now be replaced by a wider, global vision.

*T*O POSTULATE an external threat has always been a tool of the politician : 'the enemy' generates fear. As a manipulative device it permits control of an unquestioning public.

*M*ILITARY glory is the false concept that has allowed those in control to indoctrinate whole populations.

*B*OY CHILDREN throughout the nation have been taught to look to the military calling as noble and exciting.

*T*HEN, putting the nation above all laws, citizens are directed by the politicians to make war : with the ease of National rightness they fight and kill their fellow human beings.

*N*OW, communication by the world's media is undermining the glamour of the military : calling into question the rightness of the military solution.

*T*ELEVISION SHOWS both sides at war : the suffering of soldiers under command, and that of innocent civilians, seems little different regardless of military alignment.

*T*HE WORLD community finds itself objecting to the excesses of military adventuring : a wider vision starts to undermine the nationalistic view.

*F*OR THE FIRST TIME there is a global understanding that many issues once enshrined in the politics of nationhood have become supra-national.

A CALL TO ARMS is being seen in its true light by millions, as the brutal waste of life : we see that military action does not provide a solution.

*T*HE NATIONAL INTEREST is a concept of the past : it has little value in the new world order.

*T*HE DISCERNING now challenge the role of nationalism and its war-like stances : they grow rapidly in number and awareness.

THEY ARE THE NEW GLOBAL CITIZENS.

TOWARDS WORLD GOVERNMENT

RECENT WARS in the Middle East and rising concern for global security serve to increase the role of the United Nations in world government.

AS WE BEGIN to create new global administration we shall recognise, legislate and act against those who offend against Humanity and the planet.

WORLD CRIME that transcends national boundaries will be recognised for what it is : war, large scale pollution, genocide and mass destruction of natural resources are an offence against humanity.

THE UNITED NATIONS will increase its powers to develop and direct world agencies : as it does so, many issues that sit with national government today will devolve upwards.

IT IS NOW CLEAR that there is a world role for policing and law enforcement : as this grows, national armies will shrink.

WORLD SECURITY is neither the responsibility nor the right of any single nation : only concerted action against those who defy basic human rights, seek to make war, or conduct crime against the world, is appropriate.

OFTEN SUCH ACTION need not be military : for with the steady integration of the world comes greater interdependence of Nations.

FINANCE AND TRADE are no longer isolated issues within one country, for they are affected daily by world markets and their pressures.

THE effects of pollution do not respect national boundaries : one country's excesses are another's acid rain or poisoned seas.

SUCCESSFUL WORLD environmental action can only be achieved with effective world agencies in place.

PROVISION OF HEALTH, food and basic shelter are all issues that are ultimately world concerns.

WE HAVE THE POWER, the means and the resources to ensure that every human being on earth has the basic necessities and opportunities of life : only concerted world action can deliver these in practice.

THOSE GOVERNMENTS who pursue their minorities to destruction will be held to a new code of conduct which penalises such action.

THEY will eventually yield to external pressure, obliged to recognise humanitarian responsibilities as modern media puts them under the scrutiny of the world.

FOR THE TIME BEING governments continue to reinforce each others actions by their talk of national sovereignty.

SOON the world will mandate that all governments of whatever complexion have a responsibility to humanity : standards of governmental conduct will become a global requirement.

GLOBAL PERSPECTIVES will lead to acceptance that nation struggling against nation is not in their mutual interests.

A WORLD LEGAL SYSTEM will be established to administer and enforce issues of conduct by governments and heads of state : it will focus on and designate crime that transcends national boundaries.

SECURITY and guarantees of protection will be provided by the United Nations, so that small nations need not live in fear of their larger neighbours.

A COMMITMENT to world policing will give emerging or threatened countries the backing to stand up to the bullying of militaristic nations.

THE level of protection and support made available to any nation will depend on their commitment to, and progress towards democracy : no dictator or single party state will receive such protection.

FOR ULTIMATELY, it is democracy that brings freedom, and creates the preconditions for individual development.

NO International Agency will willingly protect the despot or tyrant for long.

IN TIME, all government will become a true servant to its people : not a political instrument of manipulation by an an autocratic elite.

NEW FREEDOMS and self determination will encourage expression of local characteristics and customs : the rich traditions and heritage of many regions will ensure their identities.

PEOPLE of many cultures and traditions will be appreciated for the richness of their differences : not their conforming.

AS WORLD GOVERMENT begins to take its place, equality of opportunity, as between individuals and nations, will increasingly become global.

FEAR OF NATIONALISTIC aggressiveness will recede : as it does so humanity becomes free to set new objectives, and to reach for new horizons.

COMMUNICATION AND FUTURE

NEW TECHNOLOGIES and ease of travel are linking peoples around the world : they encourage mutual understanding through communication.

TELEVISION linked to satellite provides our most powerful tool for world understanding : global news and events are delivered as they happen.

THROUGH them we recognise that those nations who once appeared as a threat have the same concerns and problems in life as we do.

FOR THE SOLUTION to many of earth's problems is shared understanding and perspective, leading to commitment to positive action.

THUS, COMMUNICATION is the key to positive change.

FREE SPEECH now crosses national boundaries at will : with increasing knowledge and freedom comes the opportunity for personal growth.

THE THREAT from other Nations will melt away, for regardless of creed, colour, race or religion we see that we are essentially all the same.

THE MORE nation sees of nation, the less they will foster aggressive intent towards each other.

THE POWER of governments to dictate to their population is steadily decreasing : communication acts to undermine political control.

NO LONGER can governments decree what people are permitted to know, or censor external events, or manage public attitudes towards other Nations.

*C*OMMUNICATION across boundaries encourages suppressed people to start thinking and sharing their thoughts without guilt : reform will be driven increasingly by these people.

*C*OUNTRY by country, populations will organise themselves and progressively withdraw their mandate to govern until the tide of reform has swept away the greatest iniquities and injustices.

*T*HE STEADY DEMISE of manipulative ideologies will be the result.

*F*EAR WILL RECEDE as the ability of communication to empower ordinary people becomes universally understood.

*B*IG BUSINESS, religion and many other organisations have become global : their structure crosses national boundaries with ease.

*H*EADS OF NATIONS can confer immediately a problem arises : the room for international misunderstanding is decreased.

*T*HE ECONOMIES of different countries are now irrevocably interlinked, fuelled by their ability to communicate easily.

*F*OR THE FIRST TIME we can monitor many aspects of the Earth and her problems from space : the international concern that is generated by this new perspective leads Nations to act in concert on global issues.

*E*ACH of these phenomena are new, driven by advancing technology and creating a shift in human awareness.

*E*ACH is a stabilising factor, encouraging unity in the world and reducing the risk of conflict : communication is integrating the World.

ABUNDANCE
& WEALTH

*A*BUNDANCE is the natural state of the universe : there are unlimited resources for us to call upon.

*U*NDERSTANDING and aligning with the energies and purpose of the universe gives access to its limitless resources : you can use them to achieve all the wealth you can possibly need.

*Y*OUR WEALTH is the sum total of all around that you value : people, relationships, material things.....and even MONEY!

*Y*OU ARE RESPONSIBLE for your own wealth generation : the universe will provide abundantly if you hold yourself open to receiving.

*T*HE EXPANSION of wealth has no limits : wealth is an infinite resource, growing through creative activity.

*D*O NOT DETRACT from the genuine wealth creators : many industries are past their time and must be replaced by new activity.

*T*HE CREATORS are the source of new employment : through them the fruits of creativity can touch and benefit many.

*T*HE most creative ideas generate new wealth and do not diminish the wealth of others : there is infinite creativity available.

*R*ESPECT the great social and economic value of those who make available the products of their creativity, and thus generate employment :their qualities are to be admired and encouraged.

*B*E WARY of the unscrupulous for there are many ways of gaining material wealth by taking from others.

*T*HOSE who live off others by cheating and manipulation become like mistletoe : a parasitic plant unable to survive without drawing from the sap of another tree.

*S*UCH non-creative methods constitute stealing and do nothing for spiritual progress or well-being.

*B*Y USING your gifts of intuition and creativity to generate wealth you can achieve comfort, satisfaction and even luxury without the disapproval of the universe.

*F*OR SPIRITUAL PROGRESS does not require you to give up worldly goods and live in poverty.

*T*O DO SO may be pious, but it is to deny the bounty of the universe which is there for your use.

*Y*OUR PURPOSE is to be the perfect blend between the physical and the spiritual. Take full advantage of both : live in and share your abundance.

INTEGRITY IN BUSINESS

EACH OF US, in some way, is in business.

BUSINESS and commerce have the express approval of the cosmos : they are vital to the well-being of humanity.

THOSE who decry business or act unthinkingly against large corporate bodies are often frightened by their apparent power or conditioned by the adverse behaviour of a small minority.

IN DEMONSTRATING concern about business excess, act with integrity and be balanced in your purpose.

DO NOT BRAND and reject all of human industry because of the wrong actions of a minority.

FOR BUSINESSES, too, are becoming aware of new attitudes and their benefits : new corporate cultures are developing as a result of increasing consciousness.

SOME MANAGERS have learnt that by acting with love and establishing common purpose they empower their staff : they understand that an inspired and motivated team is the key to success.

MANY MORE will discover enlightened ways to manage : then great gains will be made in individual commitment and effectiveness, and in corporate morale.

IN SECURING the fortunes of your business, honour your colleagues, suppliers, customers and competitors.

THE creative approach to business brings great benefit : group thinking and development of intuition contribute to success.

SEEK TO CREATE dynamic forms of group interaction and align the creative energies of all who contribute to the corporate culture.

VISION AND PURPOSE is required for success and must be a shared commitment.

TO PROFIT from creativity with integrity is entirely valid : there is no limit to imagination and what it can achieve.

FOR THE UNIVERSE has limitless creative resources available for our use.

WHILE many businesses conduct themselves with integrity and purpose there are also those that offend against humanity.

ALWAYS WORK with integrity, for profit derived from sharp practice, unfair competition, exploitation of people or the pillaging of natural resources is clearly wrong.

BRIBES, industrial espionage and threats of corporate, legal or individual abuse are a sign of a sick and failing business.

DO NOT get involved in such activities : eventually they will be repaid in kind, cause you anguish and perpetuate your long term business decline.

IF YOU WORK for those whose standards are less than your own, leave them for an environment that more closely suits you : find a business with integrity.

LOW INTEGRITY can only survive with the consent of those within the business : we are each responsible for the standards that are set in our work place.

GREATER accountability and clear corporate standards will encourage responsible action from individuals.

WHATEVER the management style a business chooses, clear leadership is essential : no business can succeed for long by committee.

A BUSINESS organised as an extended family works better, by incorporating love, high integrity and common purpose.

GOVERNMENT also has a responsibility to create and preserve a healthy environment for business : to minimise the economic changes that cause large scale redundancies.

FOR new businesses everywhere are the lifeblood of human endeavour : they offer great excitement as they develop.

IT IS VITAL that participants in new ventures understand the risk of failure : and can thus accept it without trauma if it should come.

ECONOMIC INSTABILITY in a nation is the enemy of initiative : it causes the bravest souls who have started businesses to loose their livelihood without redress.

87

A D V E R T I S I N G

*A*DVERTISING is a vital part of life : rooted in creativity, it oils the wheels of commerce.

*W*ITHOUT IT many companies and much employment would not exist.

*W*ISE USE of the media ensures communication about product and service : it facilitates business and expands consciousness

*A*DVERTISING has often come into disrepute : its use of inappropriate images, subliminal messages and misrepresentations have offended.

*T*HE OVER-USE of sexuality and macho behaviour in consumer advertising dishonours the customer and trivialises the product.

*S*UBLIMINAL IMAGERY is unethical, removing choice by involuntarily programming the response of the recipient.

*Y*ET IN A CONSCIOUS society many established images reflect our needs and desires : we choose to be influenced, and even enjoy it.

*B*Y ALL MEANS, object to misuse : but not to all advertising, which is a valuable tool to stimulating trade.

*I*T IS ONLY the few that offend : before condemning it, consider where we would be without it. The focus should be on standards.

*L*OOK AT THOSE nations that do not have the benefits of a market economy, and thus no advertising : see the food queues, the lack of choice.

*T*HEN UNDERSTAND the importance of good product promotion : the benefit of widespread distribution, and the consistency of branded goods.

INTERNATIONAL TRADE

SOME NATIONS have very different business cultures than your own : a legal offence in one country may be established business practice in another.

BEFORE SEEKING to do business with other nations, it is vital you study their business protocols.

AVOID MAKING cultural shock waves and be well briefed on local ways: if you do not, you will fail in your task.

YOU WILL inadvertently offend and fail to create a climate for success.

MANY international businesses stand ahead of governments in both resources and world perspective: their activities are an excellent catalyst for global unity.

THEIR BUSINESS activities across many national boundaries serve to unite people of many races, creeds and nationality.

THE GROWTH of world trade supports world peace, security and stability : it ensures the steady spread of wealth and employment to disadvantaged nations.

92

INDUSTRY &
ENVIRONMENT

MANY large industries have a direct and substantial effect on the environment.

THEY have many issues to address, and a difficult route forward if they are to achieve environmental responsibility.

IN CRITICISING such industries, recognise their economic importance, and the size of the task they may have to grapple with.

MANY are already making prodigious efforts to solve environmental problems.

IT DOES NOT serve us to disable those who are working for change, by weight of uninformed criticism.

TOO MANY still put profits before social consciousness : focus your efforts on those who are not trying.

FOR those organisations with great potential to pollute, public scrutiny will become ever more vigorous and penalties prohibitive.

ENVIRONMENTAL auditing will become as important as financial : proper control, measurement and public accountability will soon become mandatory.

CAREER AND
EMPLOYMENT

BUSINESS must sometimes make hard decisions about people : there are times when job losses are the only hope for corporate survival.

THOSE ORGANISATIONS who do not shed overheads and jobs when trading conditions demand face the possibility of collapse : the workforce is then sacrificed to business failure.

CORPORATE failure has an effect on people that is far worse than ensuring survival by timely surgery.

THE SAME IS TRUE when new technologies force the pace of change : failure to adapt will mean the business is over-run by its competition.

THE NEED for redundancy is highly emotive, it polarises people and can generate great personal animosity : yet the right perspective, proper planning and consultation can greatly ease the problem.

KEEP LOYALTY to your employer in proper balance in this time of rapid change : recognise that it may not always be possible for the company to be loyal to you. Do not be over-committed to them.

IT IS IMPORTANT to think for yourself : to strategise and manage your career while continuing to serve your present employer with excellence.

AN INDIVIDUAL'S reliance on their job must not be so high that its loss is automatically a life disaster : be prepared for change if it should come.

IT IS NOT WRONG to move on when appropriate, if you have made a fair contribution.

FIRST, stay for long enough to deliver a worthwhile return to your employer : this preserves your integrity with him.

PLAN TO MOVE your career every few years in order to ensure your own development : thus you avoid stagnation and dependency.

PROMOTION may well be achieved within your current workplace, but recognise that advancement is often easier with a change of employment.

A PLAN for independent career action does not excuse you from maximum effort and complete loyalty in your current employment.

WHILE remaining loyal to your employer, do not accept such a work load that it damages who you are and impacts your way of being.

UNRELENTING pressure leads only to ineffectiveness, both in work and as a human being.

A LITTLE STRESS is good, a vital ingredient in human motivation.

BUT THE MASSIVE stress of extreme over-commitment must be avoided : the individual will become ill and unbalanced, and lose perspective on the priorities of life.

FOR THIS REASON employees should not be encouraged to make a level of company commitment to the exclusion of their personal interests and relationships.

THOSE who over-commit in business to the exclusion of family and personal interests, serve neither themselves, their loved ones, nor indeed their company.

TRY NOT to take your business home and inflict the problems and pressures of the workplace on your loved ones.

FOR while home support in a crisis is vital, by constantly unloading work problems at home you will steadily decrease your support and eventually increase your difficulties.

MUTUAL SUPPORT groups can help employees stay in balance, enjoy their work and business relationships, and remain true to themselves in their private lives.

SELF EMPLOYMENT is an alternative way of being in business : it offers great flexibility but greater responsibility than being an employee.

YOU NEED great discipline to succeed on your own.

DECIDING TO WORK for yourself, or to start a new business, should be seen as a personal accolade : your new self appointment will allow you great opportunity for personal development.

IF THIS is your next move, congratulate yourself : you have risen to unemployability by discovering the joy of becoming self responsible.

YOUR independence and freedom in life will be greatly enhanced and your soul will develop accordingly.

VISITORS

THROUGH generations human-ity has experienced many shifts in understanding.

WE ONCE BELIEVED the Earth was flat : eventually, exploration showed this idea to be false. Yet many had held the flat earth theory to be an absolute.

THEN FOR A TIME we told ourselves that earth was the hub of the universe : mathematics and careful observation moved us on from this belief.

A FAR GREATER CHANGE in our perspective is soon to come : absolutes are about to be challenged.

OPEN YOUR MIND to the possibility that the Cosmos is teeming with life : our rejection of life outside the planet is like the flat earth belief.

THE BIBLE talks of angels and archangels, cherubim and seraphim : it presents a celestial structure that we do not question in a religious context.

THE BIBLICAL WORDS illustrate something specific, but written in a form for early Christians to understand.

FOR there are many forms of life beyond our world : some far in advance of humanity.

WE WERE FIRST brought to Earth by other beings who planned and monitored us through the ages : but life decisions and progress have always been solely our responsibility.

IN SPIRIT some are like us : they have merely moved on to higher planes, having learnt the lessons of incarnation in earlier times.

THERE ARE MANY others who are spirit-beings of light, never having had material form.

VISITORS from elsewhere once moved freely amongst us in physical form. Memories of them persist today as myth, folklore and legend : they were spiritually advanced volunteers.

MANY OF US were here when the visitors came : in our dreams we may sometimes remember them.

A FEW CAME from other parts of the universe and were given special responsibilities for the growth of humanity.

T HEY LEFT some of their number here to become guardians and teachers.

S OME WERE TRAPPED in the density of this earth, unable to generate the power to return home : they, like us, have now been here in human form for generations.

T HESE ADVANCED souls have gone through many lives on Earth and are now becoming activated as leaders for change.

T HE TIME FOR CHANGE is here, this part of our development is almost complete : soon, the visitors will return and both guide us and learn from us.

T HERE WILL BE a great reunion : from our ancient genetic memory we will remember who they are and the relationships we have always had with them.

T HE SUM of understanding on Earth is increasing exponentially : it is the driving force behind the shift in consciousness.

I T BRINGS irrevocable change : as humanity's knowledge expands and our own perspectives change.

A S the Millennium dawns we will gain new insight, shake off personal fear, and become infinitely more spiritual.

F OR when our gestation is complete,

HUMANITY WILL BECOME

THE PERFECT BRIDGE

BETWEEN SPIRIT

AND MATTER.

W E SHALL take up our rightful place in the universe, as was always intended.

T HE AGE OF PISCES is drawing to a close. Prophecies of old will now come to pass.

FOR AQUARIUS IS UPON US.

EARTH WARNINGS

*T*HOSE SPIRIT BEINGS who first brought us here have been charged with the planet's well-being and safety : for aeons they have been its keepers.

*F*OR THE MOMENT you may prefer to think of them as separate : although they are part of humanity, they are not in our physical form.

THIS MESSAGE IS FROM THEM :

101

THE EARTH is a living organism that reflects the wholeness and balance of the human race.

GAIA is the name given to the spirit of the living earth. She protects the stability of the planet and its environment.

IN THE PAST, GAIA has always been able to heal herself.

THE KEEPERS have been working to help maintain her balance in the face of great human abuse.

GAIA is now deeply wounded by pollution and the devastation of her natural resources : she is under ever increasing strain.

WE must act together in her defence.

THE EARTH'S GREEN MOVEMENTS are well intentioned, but Gaia cannot be healed by the action they take alone.

THEIR CONCERNS are well founded but they do not have sufficient power to succeed alone.

IN MANY PLACES their ability to be effective is diminished by their drive for social acceptability.

THE ENVIRONMENT is a personal responsibility for each of us : its improvement cannot depend solely on political movements.

IN the physical world OUR RAIN AND WATER MUST BE CLEAN and unpolluted if it is to continue enabling life.

WE MUST PROTECT and proliferate our plant and tree life : the forests are the lungs of the earth and renew the oxygen we need to live.

A GREAT INCREASE in trees is needed to match the growth in world population : yet deforestation is rampant.

A FOREST may be intensely farmed without global harm if appropriate tree replacement is a part of the programme : but forests must not be destroyed.

GREATER air pollution and the steady failure of the oxygen supply is the penalty.

NUCLEAR WEAPONS testing remains the greatest physical danger : explosions beneath the Earth's surface are straining her plates and damaging her magnetic field.

A GALACTIC chain reaction can result from one nuclear mistake, thus taking a human-generated problem far beyond the confines of Earth.

WE OPERATE nuclear systems in ignorance of their true potential for destruction.

YET from the same technology will spring a new source of power without pollution : used with care and skill it will revolutionise the power supply of the world.

BEYOND the potential for physical damage to Earth is its spiritual counterpart.

FOR GAIA is also affected by spiritual as well as physical abuse.

THERE are governments around the world that manipulate their people by fear : invoking extreme religious or political fervour and using great violence.

OTHERS ACHIEVE the same ends through propaganda and misuse of the media.

THEIR ACTIONS cause spiritual distress for humanity : the earth beneath them responds and its positive life force is depleted.

THIS is a spiritual cancer that must be eliminated so that GAIA may survive.

THE GREAT energy beings of the universe are now committed to help, and have mobilised for action.

EARTH IS THE FOCUS of attention from the highest life-forms in the Cosmos, for the human experiment has its past failures and cannot be allowed to fail again.

SUCH close attention is unique in the history of the Cosmos.

FOR EARTH is the universe's second global experiment to establish a free-will society of physical beings : the first was once founded on another planet in our solar system.

IT was known as *MALDEK.*

MALDEK developed a military society who produced nuclear weapons. In deploying them they eventually destroyed themselves.

THEIR PLANET was reduced to rubble.

ALL THAT remains of Maldek are the many small asteroids that are now the rings around Saturn.

ATLANTIS was also a reality: an early society on Earth which developed sophisticated technology.

THEY WERE given a high energy power source, based on cosmic power collection and transmission through giant crystals.

AN IDEOLOGICAL difference with their sister civilisation of Lemuria led to war. Alas, their cosmic power source was also then adapted to create powerful weapons.

GREAT devastation followed: many of Earth's desert regions today are a legacy of that conflict.

THE PLATES of the Earth's crust beneath Atlantis were ruptured, and she sank slowly beneath the surrounding ocean, taking some years to disappear.

THOSE who are charged as the keepers of Earth are now focussed on the great risk of a further catastrophe, arising once again from the impact of humanity's excess and warlike nature.

FULL OF CONCERN and sadness for Gaia and her plight, the keepers can no longer maintain her stability in the old way.

STRONGER MEASURES for GAIA'S recovery have therefore been invoked, for the areas of great negativity and global negligence on the planet must be restored to balance.

EARTHQUAKE, lightening and other natural disasters are being used like a surgical instrument : they give healing to some of the worst affected places.

THIS MAY NOT BE ENOUGH.

A MAJOR earth catastrophe on a larger scale will occur if cosmic surgery and changing human consciousness does not soon heal the planet.

IN ITS WAKE, governments will collapse and financial systems will fail: potentially many will die.

EARTH AND HUMANITY must therefore quickly learn to work in harmony. If we fail, humanity's great transition will come only after catastrophe.

THIS POTENTIAL CRISIS can only be delayed for a short time : the keepers are no longer able to protect Earth from the excesses of humanity without use of even stronger measures.

THOSE WHO TAKE STEPS to heal themselves will greatly increase their personal chance of survival : they will be in harmony with Gaia and will aid her recovery.

RAPID CHANGE in human consciousness is now under way : it will focus the world on its environmental problems, and lead us to implement effective remedies.

THE CHANGE in humanity's attitude and responsibility can be made in time : we may still avoid the apocalypse.

BUT NOT until we achieve peace and harmony with ourselves will we finally heal our planet.

HIDDEN CITIES

OPEN YOUR MIND to another new possibility : a strange tale which we may yet find to be grounded in truth.

ASK YOURSELF about Atlantis : if it did indeed exist, what became of it and its sister civilization after their great war?

THEY DID NOT simply perish but were forced into survival mode by the effects of their military excesses.

THE EARTH'S PLATES were ruptured, and large land masses began to move and sink : there was time, but no option remained but to abandon the damaged territory.

ATMOSPHERIC pollution from the continued use of powerful weapons made the world environment very difficult to survive.

A GREAT DUST CLOUD around the Earth reduced sunlight to a level that changed weather and temperature above ground dramatically.

THE POPULATION of the time chose to go underground : they had found a network of vast underground caves which could be adapted to the needs of humanity.

THE EARLY DAYS were focussed on survival : many people died in the harsh conditions above ground, before their subterranean haven was ready.

THOSE THAT survived developed an advanced society which had put aside all vestiges of war : they knew that survival was only possible if they found a new direction for their battered society.

SPIRITUALITY was recognised as the most important aspect of human development : this became the focus of their attention, and over time they became a temple society, basing all activity on spirit.

GREAT multi-level cities were established, with every facility from agriculture to generation of sun-like power.

THEY WERE interlinked by high speed vacuum tubes to form a complex subterranean nation.

THEIR SOCIAL environment became one of mutual support and unconditional love : and a high degree of trust between individuals.

THIS EXPERIENCE of interrelating in a new way triggered powers which had been previously latent : over many years the people developed to become natural telepaths, mind expanded in many directions.

THE HIDDEN CITIES from that era are said to survive and thrive to this day : and that over one hundred such colonies now exist under the earth's surface.

ITS PEOPLE have increased life expectancy to the point that no-one dies until they are ready to leave.

FOR LIKE US, they perpetually renew their body cells in a seven year cycle : but their cell replacement process provides almost perfect body regeneration.

WITHOUT THE STRESS of our kind of lifestyle they have little of the wear and tear that we see develop as old age.

They have thus achieved NEAR-IMMORTALITY.

THEY ARE technically and spiritually in advance of the best of our sciences in many ways : there is a great deal that they know which we have yet to discover.

IT IS SAID that they now wish to share this knowledge with us of upper Earth : that they have committed to integrate with our society by the turn of the 20th century.

TO SHARE their knowledge directly with us will create great problems for them : we represent a terrible risk.

OUR AGGRESSIVE way of being can destroy their longevity, and accelerate their ageing to a faster rate than ours : for they gave up defences against our type of non-spiritual human long ago.

IT IS ONLY this aggression that causes our ageing and death : this is the possibility they face if they choose to be with us.

SO WE WILL WAIT to see if they come : when they do, they may make a great sacrifice in order to communicate with us.

MIND
EXPANSION

*I*N THE MIND AND BODY there are powerful facilities which have long been latent in the human design : and are now being invoked.

*A*S THE HARDWARE for the mind, the human brain is the most complex physical structure in the universe. There is much about it still to be explored.

*T*HE MIND and our spiritual connections together have abilities we have not yet recognised : far less sought to develop.

*S*INCE we do not understand the overall design, our learning systems act to suppress rather than develop our latent abilities.

*C*REATIVITY and intuition are skills of the greatest value : yet they are largely stifled by the World's educational systems.

*A*CHIEVEMENT of a doctorate may be extremely hard work, requiring stamina, commitment and intensive research : yet it can be gained without ever developing the vital creative ability.

*T*HUS, the highest of educational awards can be achieved by merely studying cause and effect : little originality is called for.

*F*ORMAL EDUCATION does not address metaphysical qualities : yet they are the key to expanding who we are.

*T*HE DEVELOPMENT of non-scientific mental abilities in every human being is crucial to humanity's progress.

*T*HE BRAIN increases its power and develops rapidly in an environment which constantly stimulates : but if you reduce your life to routine it calcifies.

*T*HEREFORE, seek change rather than accepting long-term routine.

*S*PEND TIME in the pursuit of your personal growth, especially in matters of the spirit.

*S*TUDY with like-minded groups : debate the results with those around you : put what you have learnt into practice.

IN THE LIGHT of the changes that are now happening, it is the best investment you can make : your expanding spirituality will change who you are.

OUR CHILDREN are born with increased spiritual potential and learning capacity : the brains of the new generations show the first signs of human metamorphosis.

DISLEXIA is increasing : often, it afflicts the obviously intelligent. It is a side effect of a modified memory system, intended for learning by methods other than by rote.

THESE YOUNG ONES have a database memory organisation, yet we feed them knowledge serially : the result is confused co-ordination of the eye, hand and brain.

WE MUST CREATE a learning environment where their latent abilities can be brought out : enhanced, and the potential released.

RADICALLY NEW learning systems will become widespread and teachers will gradually abandon resistance to computers as a principal teaching device.

ELECTRONICALLY-BASED teaching systems will gradually become central to the learning process.

POWERFUL educational computers will enable teachers to become learning managers : their options for presenting knowledge will be greatly increased.

STUDENTS WILL LEARN at the pace which is best suited to them individually and in a way which holds their interest. Thus both speed and retention in learning will rise dramatically.

WE SHALL TRAIN new generations to fully explore and use the right side of the brain : and its creative and spiritual abilities.

LEARNING and mental training will start at an ever younger age : accelerated learning will speed the whole process.

A STATE OF FLOW will be used to enhance consciousness during lessons : to keep students interested and excited by their subject.

M ETHODS based on trance states will allow large tracts of detail to be absorbed rapidly and accurately.

T HE CLASSROOM will no longer be a convoy system, constrained by the speed of the slowest : new technologies will extend the scope of teaching and enhance flexibility.

T HE INDIVIDUAL'S capacity for learning will be greatly enhanced : approaching full use of the human brain in education.

E DUCATION will recognise both traditional learning skills and subjects, and the need for fundamental spiritual development so that intuition and individuality become important ingredients.

B UT IN SETTING UP the process, we need to ensure that great integrity is applied so as to avoid indoctrination.

T HE MIND EXPANSION in our children will be spectacular, once the potential is understood and appropriate technique applied : after a time it will induce the greater change predicted for humanity.

T HIS NEW GENERATION of mind-expanded people will thus make rapid progress in all fields of human endeavour, as well as human spirituality.

H UMANITY WILL GAIN the power to become spiritual at a higher level : and abandon materialism as the only goal in life, having understood that it does not provide the happiness that many now assume.

S OON these spiritual powers will be released : mysteries which today are only explored by a few eccentrics will be widely understood and embraced.

T HE NEW ERA will bring scientific understanding which will allow human pressures on the Earth's environment to be greatly reduced.

T HROUGH expanding consciousness we will all learn to manage and care for our planet.

N E W
H O R I Z O N S

HUMAN ACTION has always assumed that there are inadequate resources to provide for the world population.

MILITARY STRENGTH was seen as necessary to acquire and guard a situation of plenty.

THE STRUCTURE of nations, their authority, and most of their institutions, are based on this idea : yet the underlying assumption is fundamentally *WRONG!*

THE PROBLEMS we imagine will be solved by applying technology to create plenty : not by waging war.

AGRICULTURAL technology makes the land ever more productive : crops more resistant to disease and marginal land viable to cultivate.

NOW, WORLD HUNGER CAN BE ELIMINATED : we must act to ensure that it is.

THERE IS NO SHORTAGE of food production or growing capacity or resources : the entire world population can be well fed if we commit to so doing.

WE HAVE the ability to reverse deforestation, to push back the deserts and use them productively.

THE PROBLEM of removing hunger is now one of logistics, education, training and the financing of opportunity.

MANY OTHER breakthroughs are imminent.

*W*ITH intergovernmental co-operation, a world electrical grid will be constructed.

*S*UPERCONDUCTIVITY will provide the basis of the technology : the grid will extend to interconnect all our power generation sources.

*P*OWER STATIONS now idling for much of each day will feed continuous global demand resulting in a huge increase in generating efficiency.

*T*he grid will MORE THAN DOUBLE the power available to humanity, from existing sources.

*N*EW FORMS of housing that are self sufficient in energy and services will appear : mass production will bring their cost down below that of a new car.

*T*HESE HOMES will be easy to dismantle and replace, or move to another site : yet they will also have substance and be aesthetically pleasing.

*M*ANY accomodation problems around the world will be solved as a result.

*A*DVANCES in technology will make much fuel-burning redundant : a wholly new source of energy will be given to us, and used to solve many of the pollution problems of the planet.

*G*REAT AIRSHIPS will be designed : rigid hulled and jet powered, they will reduce the cost of transporting both goods and passengers by an order of magnitude.

*T*HEY WILL CARRY a thousand tons or more and travel at three hundred miles per hour.

*I*N THE EVENT of engine failure or structural damage the airship will drift to the ground and not fall from the sky. And their technology will be proof against fire risk.

*T*HE AIRSHIPS will solve many logistical problems in giving aid, especially in major disasters. They will remove the need for transport infrastructure.

*N*ATIONS that have for long been disadvantaged will benefit from these new possibilities, *and quickly pass the developed countries in many ways.*

NEW COMMUNICATIONS technologies will create global links for many special interest groups.

FROM THIS a new form of nationhood will evolve, based on personal interest and not geography or race : individuals will belong to several such electronic nations, simultaneously.

IT IS HUMANITY'S nature to explore : a new dimension of exploration is imminent, for it is self-evident that we have both the wish and the means to leave Earth.

AS THE Pilgrim Fathers sailed to find new lands, little caring what risk they ran, so many will seek new horizons outside this Earth.

WE SHALL plan to take to and colonise space, and build settlements under the sea.

A TIME will soon arrive when the costs of operating in space will be greatly reduced.

THE TECHNOLOGIES of war will no longer be needed : converted to developing the equipment for vigorous activity in space.

THE EXPLORATION of space will be a co-operation of nations and a not a military race.

SPACE EXPLORATION on a large scale will start to be viable : we shall grasp the opportunity and many will prepare to leave.

AS EXPERIENCE is gained and the technology becomes more familiar the colonisation of other planets will follow.

THE ISSUE is merely 'when?', for we have the technology now.

THOSE in government who promote space colonisation will gain lasting credit for the stability and new growth they bring us : an era of prosperity and excitement will be ushered in as we reach for new horizons.

THIS NEW adventure will be followed by the people of Earth with great enthusiasm and will do much to bind Nations together.

WE WILL THEN start to adapt to many new places outside Earth as permanent settlements and begin our gradual exploration of the Universe.

THE PILGRIM FATHERS will once again seek freedom in a new land.

A CALL TO ACTION

IF WE ARE TO INVOKE the great changes that are predicted and imminent, we must act with commitment : only then will the transition gain the required momentum.

IT IS NOT enough to have become highly spiritual but to remain passive : to those who have reached a settled spiritual state, a call to action is the greatest personal challenge they can receive.

WE were given dominion over the Earth when we came here. Responsibility was accepted by us aeons ago : yet now 'dominion' has been wrongly interpreted as unrestrained licence to exploit.

WE REMAIN at great risk of destroying our destiny and our planet. The alternative is to make a great leap forward.

YOU
ARE THUS
CALLED UPON
TO TAKE
ACTION

MAKE a new commitment to act for the welfare of our planet and the renaissance of humanity.

FIRST prepare yourself : urgently explore new spiritual concepts and human possibilities and be clear what you are willing to believe.

AGREE with yourself that you are not a mere follower, but here to make a difference to humanity's progress.

COMMIT YOURSELF to stand up for what you believe and take positive action.

BECOME a world citizen : dedicate your efforts and actions to humanity as a whole.

DO NOT be constrained by the barriers of your tribe, sect, colour, creed or country.

DISCUSS your beliefs widely : work to catalyse in others their interest and understanding, and their wish to explore.

118

*H*ONOUR and protect life in all its forms.

*A*CT against pollution and promote natural methods to replace violent chemical processes.

*P*USH forward attitudes and action on environmental issues and the protection and restoration of our atmosphere.

*A*CTIVELY support technological advance where it carries us forward without environmental damage or risk.

*S*EEK to ban violence - whether it be expressed as war or as personal aggression : neither has any place here.

*D*EMAND an end to military competition : the release of its huge resources to be turned instead to solving the problems of famine and food logistics.

*R*EJECT outdated concepts of national sovereignty and the support they give for isolation and aggression towards others.

*S*EEK health and education for the world, and the replacement of failed economic structures.

*A*BOVE ALL, lobby to outlaw nuclear testing ,for it is doing great internal damage to our planet : it also threatens other life forms.

*R*EMEMBER the fate of Maldek, the tenth planet : and Atlantis.

*Y*OUR greatest contribution to the great shift in consciousness is to bring others with you : stir up their imaginations and commit them too, to take action.

*F*OR a high proportion of the world's population must act in concert if things are to change for the good : understanding must now reach critical mass.

THE NEED FOR
EFFECTIVE ACTION IS
NOW MOST URGENT.

IT IS PERSONAL TO YOU.

T R A N S I T I O N

HUMANITY IS AT A CROSSROADS.

*O*UR challenge is to rise above the systems of the past : war, national sovereignty, greed for resources, and manipulative religion, all of which obscure fundamental truth.

*W*E are not yet born into our intended form, but humanity's long gestation will soon be over : the troubles of today's world are the last and severest labour pains.

*A*LL we need to do is to raise up the consciousness of the world to a level that invokes transition.

*S*PIRITUALITY is expanding around the world : as it does so there is relentless pressure and continuous movement towards positive changes.

*I*N order to help to make the change, listen, explore, question, assimilate and adjust as signs of the New Age appear around you.

*I*NVOKE your willingness to believe and have faith in what is happening, for it will be to your lasting benefit.

*B*E CLEAR on where you stand, for a clear position on issues of change will be vital.

*D*O NOT be disheartened by the warring and struggle that still appears to dominate the world : it is a positive sign.

*F*OR ANCIENT WRITINGS predict that as World transition begins, humanity will become polarised.

*W*HILE those receptive to spiritual growth are raising their understanding to a new level, the aggressive and autocratic are becoming more polarised.

THE LAST resolutions of international problems by means of war will accompany the transition : the aggressors are making their last stand.

THEY WILL SOON LOSE the control they have always had : without it centuries of world domination by the autocratic and militaristic will finally and permanently be ended.

STAND firmly against war and aggression : but also recognise the positive signs of resolution and transition that current conflict brings.

BE a world citizen and stand above the false pressures of your tribe, creed and country.

WHILE it is right to honour your roots and enjoy your heritage understand that they cannot set you above humanity at large.

BY recognising the rights of all humanity, and caring for every facet of human existence, you can only do good.

AND BY SPREADING this perspective we will soon ensure our transition to a new world understanding.

TELEVISION will increasingly accept and present spiritual issues and global attitudes. As it becomes truly global in its scope it will be a powerful instrument for positive change.

OUR changing perspective will show us that many world problems begin to be solvable.

WE will be moved to act vigorously in resolving many long-standing tragedies affecting deprived countries, or caused by military ambitions.

ISSUES of state, sovereignty and religion will be swept away as we change.

ARRIVAL

*W*E WERE DIRECTED *by Christ to go forth and multiply, and to fill the world with humanity : completion of this task was to precede the end of the age of Pisces.*

IT IS NOW DONE

*A*S *the era gathers momentum, our human design will at last become clear and begin to be fulfilled : systems and powers that you have long suspected to be latent in your body, will be invoked.*

*H*UMANITY *was created to be spiritually powerful in a material form so that the physical universe can be occupied and enjoyed. We are on a path of learning, and our next transition, when we shall expand our abilities in many ways, is close.*

*T*HE *birth of humanity into its intended form will release our great potential : for many it will come in this lifetime.*

122

FOR THE FOCUS of the great spirits of the universe is on Earth : we are their great experiment, and we are being nurtured and encouraged towards rapid change.

WE ARE DESIGNED to be the universal spirit embodied in matter, the first physical beings of completely free will : the great spirits of the universe have never experienced incarnation in physical form, and have sought to give us that gift.

WITH the positive energy the cosmos is sending us, humanity's awareness is steadily increasing : you will witness change around you continue to accelerate.

WHAT will result was always intended, and the fulfilment of humanity is now inevitable.

THE TRANSITION is not fixed in time : it will take place over a period, perhaps two or three decades. The timing depends on humanity reaching a critical mass of spirituality and understanding.

YET there will be an event which triggers our final embracing of the change : an actual day will occur when the whole world first recognises the enormity of what is happening to humanity.

ON THAT DAY you will experience drama, excitement, elation, joy and relief on a scale you have never known.

WHEN the change comes, your powers will be greatly increased and the new perspective you will attain will bring revelation.

FOR THE FIRST TIME you will know precisely who you are and why you are here.

YOU will understand the nature of those spirit beings who are the essence of humanity and who have been working to help us from outside the Earth.

*I*N COMPREHENDING how they are part of us, we will be at one with them : they will become a natural part of our future lives.

*A*S TIME PASSES you will witness the steady unfolding of the Universal Plan.

*T*HE ERA of the warlord and the autocrat will have passed away : humanity will have raised its understanding and experienced its interconnectedness.

A NEW TIME of joy, creativity and expanded being will have arrived : we shall set our sights far beyond the options of life today, and seek new horizons.

*T*HE MEEK shall indeed have inherited the Earth and will soon go far beyond it.

THEREFORE

GO FORWARD LIGHTLY

AND HAPPILY,

AND WITH A SENSE

OF OPENNESS ABOUT

ALL THAT IS

HAPPENING AROUND YOU

FOR THE GREAT NEW ADVENTURE IS BEGINNING.

AND REMEMBER........

.........YOUR HELP IS CRUCIAL

THE

END